e-mail @nd business letter writing

e-mail @nd business letter writing

lynn brittney

foulsham
LONDON • NEW YORK • TORONTO • SYDNEY

foulsham
The Publishing House, Bennetts Close, Cippenham,
Slough, Berkshire SL1 5AP, England

ISBN 0-572-02579-3

Edited by Helen Smith
Printed in Great Britain by St. Edmundsbury Press, Bury St. Edmunds, Suffolk

Contents

Introduction

At some point in life, everyone has to write business correspondence of some sort: a job application, a letter to the bank manager, an invoice to a supplier, even a complaint to the council or giving notice to a landlord. Business correspondence generates more paper world-wide than any other form of written communication: the prediction of the 'paperless office' has never been fulfilled. Even the e-mail revolution has simply generated more paper: we print out the communication appearing on our computer screens without a second thought, and download and print vast quantities of information from the Internet.

Personal letters need follow no rules – they represent total freedom to write in any way you like, about any topic and using any medium. Business letters, on the whole, must follow accepted formats in order to fulfil their function as a communication designed to perform one or more specific tasks. These may include negotiating, complaining, apologising, selling, forming a contract, and so on. Such formats are not limited to the printed letter; even e-mail now has a code of conduct, rules of etiquette by which businesses may communicate via computer. Within a business environment people feel safe with certain formats and respond better to types of communication that they recognise and accept.

You and your business will be judged by the correspondence you send, so this book offers a basic grounding in writing such correspondence to help you produce effective, well-presented letters, faxes and e-mail. The book is particularly aimed at individuals and small or new businesses, but larger businesses may still find much of help and interest.

Technology is there to help you too. These days, most computers designed for home or office use are supplied with word-processing software containing ready-made templates for business communication: such products offer one or more suitable layouts for any number of business documents you require – fax, memo, letter and invoice to mention but a few. You can even purchase business letter-writing software, which guides you through the basic requirements for each document step by step. Such software is discussed in this book, and recommendations given, but bear in mind that it is not possible to give totally specific information owing to the variety of products available and the pace at which technology moves forward.

Using this book

This book is divided into three parts.

- The first part of this book, chapters 1 through 8, is devoted to the basic principles of written business communications such as layout and style, writing and dictation techniques, the etiquette of communications both home and abroad, and the correct use of English. It also provides information on the use of technological aids such as word-processing applications, e-mail and speech/voice recognition, and when to use different types of communication such as letter, fax, and e-mail.
- The second part of the book, chapters 9 through 14, is primarily devoted to the writing of business letters. It contains suggestions for how to start and finish letters well, and contains examples of suitable letters to solve specific business requirements. For example, you will find information about letters between employer and employee; awkward or difficult letters; and letters from one business to another. You are unlikely to always find the exact letter to suit your purpose on every occasion, but the examples provide guidance as to the correct tone and style to adopt and a framework on which to base a letter, and the notes within the chapters should help you to adapt them to your needs. Your letters should always suitably represent you and your business, so you will want to inject some of your own personality into them in any case.
- The third part of the book is a reference section containing appendices of useful information. This includes the correct

way to address titled persons; a list of common punctuation, typing and proof correction marks; and lists of words and phrases that often cause trouble for the writer.

The examples given in this book are, of course, all imaginary, as are the names and addresses used. They do not include letters of a strictly legal nature that may need to be cited in litigation, for obvious reasons. Some guidelines are provided on writing letters of a legal nature – letters of employment and dismissal, for example – but as a rule you should never write a letter that may be used in a court of law without first seeking professional legal advice.

Acknowledgements and thanks

This book uses examples from, shows pictures of and refers to the following products, both of which are licensed products of and registered trademarks of the Microsoft Corporation:

- Microsoft® Word 97
- Microsoft® Outlook Express 5

Other licensed products, companies and websites are also referred to in the text of this book, and these include trademarked products and names.

The trademarks and ownership of all products, companies and websites mentioned in this book are recognised and acknowledged by the writers and publishers of this book.

Thanks are due to various translation companies for their assistance with the chapter *International correspondence.*

CHAPTER 1

First impressions count!

Whatever the document, giving a good impression starts with the basics: paper and ink, or print. Finely honed text is all very well, but if it is badly printed or on scruffy, thin or unsuitable paper, all your efforts will be wasted. This is less of a problem with technological communication but even here the use of unsuitable typefaces, colour and graphics can cause the recipient of your carefully composed communication to consign it to the electronic dustbin.

In this chapter, we look at two things: using quality paper and ink or its electronic equivalent to give the best first impression; and selecting the best format for your communication.

Think quality

Making a good impression starts with paper, ink, and the design of your communication. There are a number of aspects to consider.

Paper quality

Business notepaper should be of good quality. Paper suitable for letters is often described as 'Bond' or 'Script' and is classified according to its weight in grams per square metre – usually shown as g/m^2, or simply as grams. A weight of 70-90 g/m^2 is suitable for most purposes, but if you are using a computer printer make sure that you select paper of a weight and texture that your printer can cope with. Many of the printers available today – inkjet printers in particular – cannot print on paper with a rough texture or degree of stiffness, or on very thin paper. (Thick paper can also cause paper jams, especially if you are printing a series of letters at speed.) Similarly, it does not give a good impression if your business communication is printed on photocopier-weight paper, which is a cheap alternative that does not absorb printer ink well – especially noticeable when using colour and images. Even if you have not photocopied the communication, the impression is that it is mass-produced and therefore not a personalised message for the individual to whom it is addressed.

Paper size

Paper of A4 size (210mm x 297mm) is most commonly used in business these days, in Britain and most of Europe at least – some American and Asian organisations continue to use Letter size (8.5in x 11in), which was previously the norm, but this is becoming less common. A4 allows adequate space for most letters and is best suited to standard envelope sizes, and most computer software assumes this is the size you want to use: templates for memos, faxes and letters are invariably based on A4 paper. A small stock of A5 paper (half the size of A4) is useful, particularly if you regularly send notes that are short and to the point.

Headed notepaper

Nearly all businesses, and many private individuals, have a printed letterheading on their paper. Like all other parts of the letter, the heading should present a suitable image, and give all the necessary relevant information. It is possible to purchase (primarily from stationery superstores) stationery containing your choice of graphic art – all you have to do is select the graphics you prefer and design your address format on the computer so that it will print on the ready-designed paper. Most word-processing and desktop-publishing software these days contains a graphics or WordArt library from which you can import images or fancy text into your document to make up your own letterhead. Some examples of such graphics and WordArt are shown on the next page; these are from Microsoft Word™.

Figure 1: Typical word-processor graphics

On letterheads, all businesses should for obvious reasons include the business name and address and telephone number, plus the fax number and e-mail address if you have them. Depending on the legal status of your business it may be necessary also to include other information – for example, a private limited company (Ltd) must show its registration number, registered office address and the names of its directors on its letterheaded paper, and if registered for VAT, the VAT registration number must also be shown. You should always check the precise requirements with your accountant and, if necessary, solicitor. In some cases it may also be useful to include a brief description of the business somewhere on the letterheading if it is not apparent from the company name, for example, R Johnson & Sons is not very informative; R Johnson & Sons (Builders) is much more helpful.

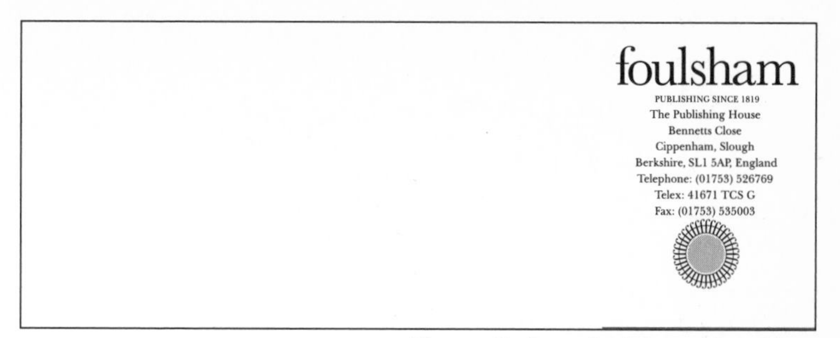
foulsham
PUBLISHING SINCE 1819
The Publishing House
Bennetts Close
Cippenham, Slough
Berkshire, SL1 5AP, England
Telephone: (01753) 526769
Telex: 41671 TCS G
Fax: (01753) 535003

Figure 2: A typical letter-heading

Continuation sheets

Don't forget when ordering or designing headed notepaper that you will almost certainly need some continuation sheets – plain sheets of paper in a matching weight and colour – on which you can continue your letter should it run to more than one page. Some people use a lighter weight paper for continuation sheets but having equal weight paper gives an impression of quality and attention to detail.

Envelopes

If you really want to impress and make your company's communications stand out from the others, you will select envelopes that match the colour and weight of your letterheaded paper. However, there may be practical reasons why you do not. You may prefer to send invoices in manila envelopes, for example, or mailshots in window-envelopes so that addresses can be easily checked by the mail room. Similarly, letters with several enclosures may need to be in extra-strong envelopes that cannot be matched to your other stationery.

Ink and print

Ink used to be a very important subject when business letters were hand-written. It used to be considered that letters written in blue or black ink were acceptable, while coloured inks were impolite: ladies were allowed to get away with writing in purple or dark green but businessmen were not. Today the whole spectrum of colour is available to anyone with a computer and colour printer. You could print each paragraph of a letter in a different colour if you so wished. However, from a practical point of view, coloured inks do not help readability – for example, a block of red text on white paper is very difficult to read. Sales letters are sometimes designed and printed in certain colours with a view to being eye-catching and memorable. Most business communications, though, are required to convey the impression of serious business intent and therefore black text would appear to be the norm.

Typefaces

If you are using word-processing software, you will probably also have a wide selection of typefaces or fonts available to you. Some of these are acceptable for business use; others are designed purely for graphic design, for fun use, or for specific types of document. It is always best, especially when sending a document as a fax or e-mail, to stick with a typeface that is in common use, and with which your reader will be familiar. The most common at the time of writing are Helvetica (or Arial), and Times (or Roman). Remember, you are writing a business document and the importance lies in its content, not in a flashy typeface.

If you are writing long documents, such as reports, it is worth knowing that most people find serif type (such as Times) easier to read than sans-serif (such as Arial). Therefore follow the style adopted by many newspaper, magazine and book publishers, and opt for serif typefaces for text, and sans-serif typefaces for headings (as in this book).

Use the most appropriate format

These days there are so many different ways to communicate. How do you select the correct one for each occasion? Here are a few pointers.

The letter

A few years ago, the letter was the only alternative to the face-to-face business meeting. Then came the telephone, followed by an ever-increasing range of technological solutions that often are out of date before we even know how to use them – who, these days, uses telex, teletex, telegrams or telemessages for everyday communication? Now we are in the electronic information age – yet the letter remains the main tool for business communication. Why is this?

The speed, ease and cheapness of making a telephone call may have destroyed the art of private correspondence, but the same cannot be said for business correspondence. For every business telephone call made there seems to be a need to issue a piece of paper to formalise the conversation, whether it is the making of an appointment or the booking of a hotel. This, of course, is the advantage of letters, that they provide a complete written record for future reference – particularly important where money is involved.

Letters still have the edge over faxes and e-mail when it comes to being used in evidence in a court of law, because they are signed. An unsigned fax or e-mail could be created and sent by anyone wishing to impersonate another individual. The only advantage that faxes and e-mail have over letters is that they provide a record of the exact time they were sent and therefore could be used in court as evidence if the time of despatch or receipt was in dispute.

The telephone call

The telephone is very useful as a starting point in business communications. It provides the next best thing to face-to-face discussions because each person can hear the other's voice, and from that gauge their mood and transmit suitable emotion in the voice accordingly. The telephone is quick and cheap but, as we mentioned earlier, it always needs to be backed up by written communication.

The fax

Faxes are still regarded by many, particularly those engaged in international business, to be the preferred way of doing business. The Japanese specifically developed the fax machine because it allows them to send letters quickly in their own language, whether written or typed. The same applies to other nationalities that do not use the standard alphabet. Until the development of e-mail, the fax machine was also the only way to quickly send graphics. If it was essential that a customer in a remote location needed to see blueprints, photos or diagrams as fast as possible, fax was the only way to do it. Many business transactions that are time-sensitive and confidential, such as banking operations, are still conducted by fax.

E-mail

E-mail, of course, is the latest revolution. During the last few years of the 20th century the use of e-mail exploded. It combines the speed and cheapness of the telephone with the graphics capabilities of the fax and more. It is possible to send colour images and even video camera footage by e-mail. However, even this latest technology has its drawbacks. Some e-mail products cannot handle documents or attached files that are too large or too complicated, so occasionally the basic message arrives at its destination without the attachments, although this is becoming less common with the latest versions. There is no guarantee when an e-mail will arrive (rather like traditional mail in some countries): in theory it should be instant but sometimes, if traffic on the internet is very heavy, your e-mail may be placed in a queue and not arrive for 24 hours or longer. Very occasionally messages just go missing, become garbled or go to the wrong address, usually due to human error on the part of the sender or recipient. In fact any combination of human and technological error can occur. However, the biggest drawback with e-mail is the lack of privacy. You cannot reliably send confidential material via e-mail because of the risk of someone hacking into it en-route.

All these problems are slowly being solved, but meanwhile e-mail remains a somewhat inadequate method for important or secure material. If you can live with the slowness of the mail service then sending an important, valuable, confidential or bulky document still needs to be done the old-fashioned way: even then it is always wise to pay the extra for a guaranteed tracked delivery, especially if sending mail overseas. In some cases a commercial courier service may be a cheaper and safer alternative.

CHAPTER 2

Structure, layout and style

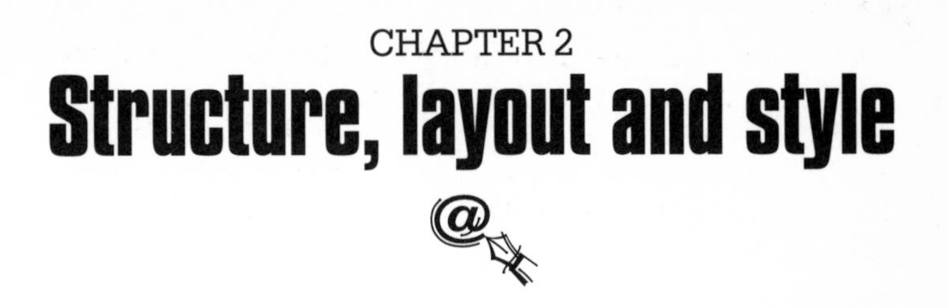

Although there is no one correct way to structure or lay out a business communication, it is important to develop an attractive and consistent style, and one that your reader finds easy to read and understand. In this chapter, we look at the basic framework of each of the three main types of business communication used today – letter, fax, and e-mail – describing each part as well as the layouts most commonly used for each, and giving some tips on style where appropriate.

For details of how to implement the structures and layouts shown here if you use a computer, see the chapter *Technology for communication*.

Business letters

Letters have the most rigid structure, layout and style of any of the types of business communication described in this book. While these may vary from one country to another (see the chapter *International correspondence*), the details in this section apply to most English-speaking countries, and are used universally within the UK.

The basic structure of a letter

Business name
Sender's address

(note: this information is often replaced by a printed letterheading)

Reference code

Date

CLASSIFICATION

TYPE OF DESPATCH METHOD

Recipient's name
Recipient's address

FOR THE ATTENTION OF

Opening greeting (salutation)

SUBJECT HEADING

Main body of letter

Complimentary close

Company's name
Sender's name
Sender's position/department name

Enclosures line

Copies line

Figure 3: The basic structure of a letter

The parts of a letter

The various parts of the letter, as shown in Figure 3, follow specific formats. These are described in detail below.

Postal addresses

In Britain, the recommended form of postal address has the post town in block capital letters; followed by the county with an initial capital only; followed by the postcode using capital letters.

For international communications, follow the conventions of that country for the recipient's address: they all differ, so use previous correspondence to that country as a guide. Don't alter the format of your own address to suit the international style. In all cases, show the country name as the last line of the address.

Reference code

Reference codes are used in letters to help in filing or to indicate the names of people writing and typing the letter (for example, BJE/glm). However, letters are often filed according to the recipient's name or organisation, which is already included in the rest of the letter, and there is no point in adding a reference code just to make the letter look more businesslike.

The reference code is usually given in the form 'Ref', 'Ref:' or 'Ref.' at the top left of the letter. If you are replying to correspondence that included a reference code you should reply as follows:

Our ref:
Your ref:

Date

Always write the date in full and not in the form of numbers alone. This is because in the UK the day is shown first, whereas in the United States and some other countries the month is shown first. Therefore 8.12.2000 could be read as 8th December or 12th August. It is also much clearer not to abbreviate month names or years. The year should always be included as it may be important for both you and the recipient if you need to refer back to your correspondence in the future. Avoid using the term 'Date as Postmark' as the envelope is usually soon discarded, especially where companies have a post room that opens the mail and just delivers the letters to the recipients, so no one will know exactly when it was sent.

The common forms for the date in the UK are 8 December 2000 or 8th December 2000.

Classification line

If your letter is personal and/or confidential, indicate this at the top left of the letter. Use 'PERSONAL' if the letter must be opened by the recipient only; a 'CONFIDENTIAL' letter may be opened by his or her deputy but should, of course, be treated confidentially. 'PERSONAL AND CONFIDENTIAL' may be used together if it is imperative that only the recipient opens the letter and acts upon it. The words are usually typed in capital letters and/or underlined. Repeat this information on the envelope.

Despatch method

Sometimes it may be useful to indicate the despatch method to be used, such as: Recorded Delivery, Registered Post, Airmail, or Courier Delivery. Type this in capitals at the top left of the letter; a pre-printed sticky label may be used instead.

Recipient's name

If possible you should include the name of an individual recipient or, at least, a specific job title. This makes the letter someone's particular responsibility and, hopefully, leads to a quicker reply. It may also be useful if you need to follow up the letter and want to know to whom you wrote in the past. However, as an alternative the name of the department and organisation, or just the organisation, may be given here. Sometimes a letter may say 'All communications should be addressed to ...', and in this case you should obviously follow instructions.

There are conventions for addressing each.

An individual

As a guide to use of first names and/or initials, follow the recipient's preferred style as indicated by past correspondence. Always use a courtesy title, and copy the spelling of names carefully.

The most common courtesy titles are Mr, Mrs, Miss and Ms. The title Esq (short for Esquire), which indicated the status of 'gentleman' in the past, may be used instead of Mr but not with it: for example, use either Mr J Brown or J Brown Esq. Note that Esq can only be used if you know the first name or initial, so Mr is generally the best courtesy title to use for most male correspondents. If a woman has indicated her preferred courtesy title on previous correspondence, you should use this. If not, and you are unsure as to her marital status, it is generally acceptable to use Ms.

In certain situations you may be unsure of the sex or status of a correspondent, particularly if you are corresponding for the first time with someone that you have not spoken to and who has not indicated these details in their correspondence. This is especially so with foreign names or names that can be used for either male or female, for example Lesley or Sam. If you cannot ask someone who knows the individual personally, then simply address them by their full name, without a courtesy title. It is quite permissible to address correspondence to, say, 'Mabusak Randwhala' or 'Lesley Smith'; this is less likely to cause offence than an incorrect assumption of male or female, or of incorrect marital status. If this seems too informal, use the salutation 'Dear Sir or Madam' to balance it.

Other courtesy titles refer to qualifications, professions or honours. Examples include:

Doctors: Dr or Doctor can be used for a man or woman and is used for persons holding a doctoral degree as well as medical doctors. Most consultant surgeons traditionally prefer the title Mr. Some medical doctors prefer the letters MD after their name: do not use both Dr and MD.

Knights: Knight's names should always include their first name (not initial) and surname. For example: Sir John Smith not Sir J Smith.

Clergy: Protestant or Anglican clergy should be addressed as The Rev J (or John) Smith, not Rev Smith; Catholic clergy as Fr John Smith (short for Father); nuns as Sr Mary (short for Sister), with any job description added afterwards, such as Sr Julia, Mother Superior.

Certain religious designations such as bishop and archbishop have their own specific titles; these are listed in

Appendix 1 together with titles, forms of address and appropriate opening and closing lines for various religious, military and royal titles.

Sometimes letters denoting honours, qualifications or professions may be used after the name. Indeed, some people insist on it and they will indicate so by always using them on their own outgoing correspondence. There are accepted rules for the order in which these are given. If a person has a number of 'letters' it is usual to use only one or two of the most high-ranking ones, and university degrees or professional qualifications are not usually included unless they are particularly relevant. For example, you may add ARIBA to an architect's name when writing to him in his professional capacity, but you would be unlikely to add BSc to your landlord's name just because you knew he had a degree.

If there is likely to be any confusion between a father and son who have the same first and surnames then it is possible to add Snr (senior) after the older man's name or Jnr (junior) after the younger man's name. It is a common practice in the USA but elsewhere some men may baulk at such a designation. In France it is common to use M. (monsieur) Andre Rouge, Pere (father) or M. Andre Rouge, Fils (son). Another solution is to use the man's job title to show which man is to receive the letter, for example, John Smith, Chairman or John Smith, Managing Director.

A job title or department name

In both these cases an organisation name should be included as part of the address, as the address to which you are writing could be home to a several companies, situated in the same building and using a communal post room; therefore there could be several, say, personnel managers. So the correct form would be Mr John Smith, Personnel Manager, Avco Tools plc.

An organisation

In most cases, the organisation's name should be given as the version used in your correspondent's letterheading, including any designation of status, such as Ltd or plc. If writing to a partnership the form 'Messrs Price & Green' is correct.

Recipient's address

This should be copied carefully from the previous correspondence if available and should be the same as the address to be used on the envelope. Avoid using abbreviations for road or town names, although it is acceptable to use the standard county abbreviations.

Addresses should include:

1. The house or building number (and a flat, chamber or office number if appropriate). No comma is needed after the number before the road name. Avoid using just a house name if possible, and do not use inverted commas round house names.
2. The road name.
3. The village name, or a district of a town if there are several streets of the same name in a town.
4. The postal town (officially called the Post Town). This is the town where letters are sorted for local delivery. The Post Town name should be given in capital letters.
5. The county – unless the town is a major city or shares the name with the county (for example: Gloucestershire should not follow Gloucester).
6. The postcode. This consists of two blocks of letters and numbers, the first block indicating a major area of the postal town, the second identifying the address down to a group of 15 or so houses, or even in some cases an individual firm's offices. There should be no punctuation in postcodes. If you are unsure of a postcode, call the Royal Mail's postcode information line on 0845 711 1222, and give the address. For the price of a local call, obtaining the postcode will help to speed up the delivery of your letter.
7. If international, the country name, in English.

Each of these parts of an address is normally given an individual line and they should be given in the order listed above. However, inside the letter the district and town names, or town and county names may share a line (separated by a comma or extra space), or, more commonly, the postal town and postcode, or county and postcode, share a line (separated by between two and six spaces).

In foreign addresses both the postal town and the county/state are usually capitalised, and zip or postal codes should always, of course, be included. Further information on addressing international correspondence is given in the chapter *International correspondence*.

'For the attention of' line

This line, which is traditionally placed between the recipient's address and the opening greeting, is used when only the name of a department or organisation has previously been given for the recipient. The usual wording is 'For the attention of Mrs J King' (underlined with no full stop) and an attention line should be used as an alternative to, not as well as, a recipient's name or job title. The 'attention' line can also be placed immediately before the recipient's department or organisation and in the fully blocked style (described later in this chapter) is often typed in capital letters and not underlined.

Opening greeting (or salutation)

The form of salutation used should be related to the way the recipient's name has been given in the address (see above); there are particular rules for royal, military, or religious personages, or those in public office (these are shown in Appendix 1). Salutations are discussed in detail in the chapter *Making a start*.

In general, the best guideline is to consider how you would address the individual in person and use that form.

Subject heading

It is often helpful to both the sender and the recipient to give a subject heading immediately after the opening greeting. It should be short and concise and should match that given by your correspondent if you are continuing discussion of the same topic. The subject heading may quote an important reference number, such as an invoice or order number. It should be underlined (in the fully blocked style it is often typed in capital letters instead) and have no final full stop. For example:

'Delivery of goods for order no 192746'

or

'INVOICE NUMBER ABC/156181'.

The main body of a letter

Sometimes it is difficult to think of suitable words with which to start the letter. Some are suggested in the chapter *Making a start*. In general, you should always refer to any previous correspondence in the first paragraph and also try to get to the point of the letter reasonably quickly.

If a letter is long and complicated it may be useful to number points or to use paragraph headings, indicating them with capitals or underlining, although this can make the letter look rather formal. It is always best to start a paragraph with a topic sentence, introducing the subject of the paragraph, as this will help your reader to follow your train of thought. However, if the letter has more than one main subject it may be worth considering sending two separate letters as this will make it easier for both your recipient and you to consign them to the appropriate person and/or files.

Try to make the final paragraph positive and state what you hope the recipient will do. Some examples are given in the chapter *Signing off*. Include a personal pronoun in final statements, for example, 'I hope to hear from you soon' rather than 'Hoping to hear from you soon'.

Complimentary close

This should match the opening greeting. 'Yours sincerely' or 'Yours faithfully' will be appropriate in nearly all cases; other closes may be used for letters to friends, or to persons of title. See the chapter *Signing off* for details.

Company name

This indicates that the letter is on behalf of the company as a whole, even though it has been written and signed by a certain individual. The business name should always be given here if the plural 'we' has been used in the main body of the letter. The company name is placed on the line immediately following the complimentary close and is usually in the form 'G Jones & Co' or 'for G Jones & Co'. If the person signing is an authorised signatory of the business, the form 'per pro' or 'pp G Jones & Co' may be used.

Signature

Letters will usually bear the signature of the writer; however, sometimes other conventions are followed. A partner signing for his firm, for example, should use the firm's name without adding his own name. Sometimes a proxy signature may be necessary, for example when the writer is not available to sign urgent letters. In this case one of the expressions used below would probably be appropriate.

J. Jones
for Marketing Director

J. Jones
for F. Reed,
Marketing Director

J. Jones
Secretary to Mr F. Reed

A firm's rubber stamp in place of a signature is generally regarded as rather discourteous. Even for circular letters it is usually possible to include a printed or duplicated signature.

Sender's name

Unless you are confident that your signature is readable, or it will be very familiar to your correspondent, it is as well to include your name immediately below the signature. This should match the signature in terms of use of first names or initials. If just initials are given the recipient will probably assume the writer is a man; in any case it is helpful if a woman adds Mrs, Miss or Ms to the name to show the style of address she prefers.

Sender's office or department

This should be added, if appropriate, on the line following the name.

Enclosures

The abbreviation 'Enc' (or 'Encs', 'Encs -', or 'Enc:') is useful both to remind you to check that all enclosures are included, and to remind the recipient that enclosures are present. Sometimes a label is used instead, but this is less common now due to the use of word-processors and computers.

Copies line

If a letter is written to a certain person but is sent for information to others, it is helpful to all concerned to indicate who has been sent copies by using wording such as:

Copies to Mr J Edwards,
Mrs R Richards

The copy for each individual can be marked by a tick against the name to save any confusion when sending the letters out.

Sometimes the abbreviation 'cc' is used in place of 'copies to', though in fact this relates to rather outdated technology; 'cc' stands for 'carbon copies' from the days when carbon paper was used to produce copies of typed letters. Similarly, you may see 'bcc' on some letters. Use this if you do not want the recipient to know who has received copies: 'bcc' stands for 'blind carbon copies' – information hidden from the main recipient but shown on the copies. For example, 'bcc Mr J Edwards' would appear on Mr Edwards' copy of the letter, but not the copy sent to the addressee.

Postscripts

Try to avoid postscripts in letters. If your letter has been well planned as suggested in the next chapter, last-minute thoughts and additions should be unnecessary.

Creating letter parts on a computer

Most standard word-processing software now has functions that can automatically insert text such as opening greetings, complimentary closes, despatch instructions, classifications and references. This usually involves selecting a menu option to choose the item you require, or in some cases, recognition by the software of the word or phrase as you begin to type it (it may then offer to complete it automatically). However, such software cannot yet tell you which is the most appropriate greeting, term or phrase for the letter you are writing!

Common letter layouts

There are three main layouts used in business letters; fully blocked, semi-blocked and fully indented. We will look at them in order of popularity and formality.

Fully blocked layout

This layout has been heavily influenced by American and European usage and therefore is ideal for international communications. 'Fully blocked' means that paragraphs are not indented and a double line space is put between each paragraph. Everything – even the signature block – is ranged to the left-hand side of the page.

42 Botley Close
Colebourn
RIPON
Yorks
R18 7QS

Your Ref 5/12A

17 May 2000

Messrs Brown & Page (Builders)
28A Long Lane
RIPON
Yorks
R12 1AN

Dear Sirs,

QUOTATION FOR EXTENSION AT 42 BOTLEY CLOSE

Thank you for your estimate dated 5 May 2000.

I am sorry to have to tell you, however, that the figure quoted is in excess of others that we have received and we shall therefore not be pursuing the matter further with you.

Thank you for supplying the quotation, nevertheless.

Yours faithfully,

John Smith

John Smith

Figure 4: Fully blocked letter layout

The above example also has what is known as an 'open punctuation' style; basically, it uses minimal punctuation. No punctuation is used outside the main text of the letter unless essential for sense (for example, if the town and county names in an address are put on the same line they should be separated by a comma or two spaces). Dates are shown without –st or –th endings, and no full stops are used in abbreviations, contractions or acronyms (for example, Mr Jones, NATO, BSc or MP).

Semi-blocked layout

This represents a compromise between the 'fully blocked' and the 'fully indented' style, in that some indentation is used for the main body of text. It is considered a little old-fashioned, nevertheless many established companies in the UK and parts of Europe prefer it as their correspondence style, along with what is called 'closed punctuation'. An example is shown below.

42 Botley Close,
Colebourn,
RIPON,
Yorks,
R18 7QS.

Your Ref: 5/12A

17th May 2000

Messrs Brown & Page (Builders),
28A Long Lane,
RIPON,
Yorks,
R12 1AN

Dear Sirs,

Quotation for extension at 42 Botley Close

Thank you for your estimate dated 5th May 2000.

I am sorry to have to tell you, however, that the figure quoted is in excess of others that we have received and we shall therefore not be pursuing the matter further with you.

Thank you for supplying the quotation, nevertheless.

Yours faithfully,

John Smith

John Smith

Figure 5: Semi-blocked letter layout

You will note that in the above example the paragraphs have been indented, but there is still a double line space between each paragraph. Punctuation has been added to the peripheral parts of the letter: the addresses all have commas at the end of each line; the reference has a colon to separate the number from the words; the date has –th added; and the salutation 'Dear Sirs' is followed by a comma. In the main body of the letter, the subject heading is in upper and lower case letters and is underlined, rather than being in capital letters only. The signature block has been moved away from the left-hand side of the page.

Fully indented layout

This style, which involves graded indentations of all the parts of the letter, has largely been abandoned since the advent of the electric typewriter, since it involved setting up lots of complicated tabs to create all the different indents. It is now primarily used for hand-written letters only, but it is worth looking at an example to show how it differs from the other layouts.

As you can see all the indents are stepped, even the signature block. This is very time-consuming to do on a typewriter, word-processor or computer, hence its fall from popularity.

42 Botley Close,
Colebourn,
RIPON,
Yorks,
R18 7QS

Your ref: 5/12A

17th May 2000

Messrs Brown & Page (Builders),
28A Long Lane,
RIPON,
Yorks,
R12 1AN

Dear Sirs,

Quotation for extension at 42 Botley Close

Thank you for your estimate dated 5th May 2000.
I am sorry to have to tell you, however, that the figure quoted is in excess of others that we have received and we shall not, therefore, be pursuing the matter further with you.
Thank you for supplying the quotation, nevertheless.

Yours faithfully,
John Smith
John Smith

Figure 6: Fully indented letter layout

A few words about envelopes

The envelope provides the first impression of your letter, so it is important that it should be neatly typed. The wording of the address should be as given in the letter. The normal convention is to type the address lengthwise along the envelope, leaving the opening in long envelopes to the left. The address should start about halfway down the envelope, leaving at least 40mm or so above for the stamp and postal frank.

The post town should be given in capitals and all parts of the address should have separate lines as this makes it easier for the postal services to deal with the letter quickly and efficiently, especially where mechanised sorting is used. The postcode should always be the final line (except for overseas letters).

Any classification such as 'PERSONAL' or 'CONFIDENTIAL' should be indicated on the envelope (a couple of lines above the name and address) and you should also indicate, by typing or using sticky labels at the top left of the envelope, the postal service to be used (First Class, Recorded Delivery, Airmail, for example) especially if the letter will be posted by someone else or dealt with in a mail department.

With larger envelopes and packages, which tend to be more prone to damage in the post, it is particularly important to include the sender's address both on the outside and inside of the package so that it can be returned if necessary – for example if the recipient's address label comes off or becomes unreadable. The sender's address should be clearly differentiated from the recipient's address by its position and size and/or use of the word 'From'.

Faxes

Faxes are generally less formal than letters, so have a less rigid structure. There is, however, a preferred structure and content for the initial page of a fax (cover page), because it is essential to provide certain information both for the recipient and in case the fax goes astray due to misdialling. This includes the date, time of transmission, sender's name and company, recipient's name and fax number. While the appearance and order of information may differ slightly from one sender to another, the way in which it is laid out, including the use of labels, is generally the same. Typical layouts are shown below.

facsimile transmission

To:	*Name of individual/position/company*	Fax:	*Recipient's fax number*
From:	*Your name/position/company*	Date:	*Today's date*
Re:	*Subject of fax*	Pages:	*The number of pages this fax runs to (including this cover sheet)*
CC:	*Name/s of those to whom the fax will be copied*		

☐ Urgent ☐ For Review ☐ Please Comment ☐ Please Reply ☐ Please Recycle

Type main body of text here.

Figure 7: A typical fax layout (1)

It is not considered necessary to have a signature block, or even to sign the message. However, many people do like to sign the bottom of the text and to use a less formal complimentary close such as 'Regards'.

FAX

To:	John Jones	Date:	03 March 2000
Company:	Jones, Smith & Jones	Your ref:	013/JJ/WD
Telephone:	083 6242735	Our ref:	INV7755
Fax:	083 6242736	No. pages:	1
Subject:	Invoice query		

John,

Further to our conversation earlier, here is a copy of our invoice 7755 for payment.

Regards,

Jane Thomson

From: Thomson, Gerald & French
Tel: 083 8263523 in case of query

Figure 8: A typical fax layout (2)

The parts of the fax as shown above are self-explanatory, except perhaps the number of pages category. It is important to put the total number of pages a fax runs to, otherwise the recipient will not know how many pages he or she should be receiving, as it may not be obvious from the text.

The boxes shown in the above example are an optional extra. Some companies like to give instructions to the recipient in this form.

Second and subsequent pages of a fax need follow no such structure or layout. They are usually easily identifiable as being connected with the cover page by the information automatically printed on each page by the fax machine. This usually includes the telephone number from which the fax was sent, and sometimes the name of the sending company.

E-mail

The basic structure of an e-mail message

There are two parts to an e-mail message: the text you type on your screen, for which there few defined rules (this is discussed more fully in the chapter *All about e-mail*); and the 'header' information, written by the e-mail software when the message is sent and en-route, which provides details of the sender, routing, date and time of transmission and receipt, and other more technical information. These days most e-mail software hides this header information from automatic view – it makes little sense and is of little use to the average user – but there is normally an option you can select to view it if you need to; for example, if you need to determine the time the message was originally sent. Consult the instruction manual for your e-mail software if you need to find this information.

Some examples of e-mail messages are provided in chapter 6.

Guidelines on layout and style

E-mail is generally recognised as a less formal form of communication, and there are few rules about layout, although style and content follow a more definite trend (these issues are covered in the chapter *All about e-mail*). However, the very nature of electronic text lends itself to a blocked rather than indented format. Postal addresses are rarely shown; dates are automatically generated; even salutations and complimentary closes are often dropped. The actual appearance of the text, including size and spacing, depends primarily on whether the e-mail is written in plain text or specially formatted text known as HTML (HyperText Markup Language – the programming language used to format documents for the Internet): most e-mail software these days can handle either format, but most messages are still sent in plain text. Plain text allows no emphasis other than capitals, and is basically the electronic equivalent of a typewriter: HTML allows bold, italics and underlining, colour, and in-line graphics. However, as not all e-mail users can read HTML documents it is generally best to stick with plain text unless you know for certain that the recipient can view what you are sending in the same format.

While you cannot physically sign an e-mail message with a pen, most people have an 'electronic signature' that they apply to each message. This can include a graphic of their signature, but more commonly just comprises their name and contact information such as e-mail address, telephone and fax number. Some include a motto or favourite quote as part of this 'signature', presumably to make it more personal. Some e-mail applications have a 'digital signature' function, which is a security feature that prevents others from reading confidential mail but requires that both sender and recipient have a 'digital ID'. If your e-mail software offers this function, it will be fully described in the user manual or on-line help.

Further information on e-mail functions and content is given in the chapter *All about e-mail*.

CHAPTER 3

Writing well

Before you put pen to paper and actually write your correspondence, give some thought to the best use of language. Language is not only the expression of a thought pattern, it is also a means of communication.

This chapter is about formulating clearly understandable ideas. Most people believe it is easy for us to understand each other so long as we speak the same language. Daily experience teaches us something else.

Communicate clearly

Nothing is easier than to express oneself in a complicated manner, and nothing is more difficult than to express oneself clearly. This is a problem for many of us, and not just a modern problem either; the poet and author Horace (65–8BC) expressed how we all feel when he wrote 'It is when I struggle to be brief that I become obscure'. These days it is most noticeably judges, politicians and scientists who repeatedly demonstrate the problem. Using language in a written communication that appears to be quasi-legal and designed to intimidate certainly achieves that effect but also leads to confusion. For example:

'I should like to express in no uncertain terms that I am in total and absolute agreement with the decision presented.'

Surely 'I welcome the decision' expresses the same sentiment in simple and easily understandable language! Yet most people, particularly in the business world, find it difficult to simplify in this way. The main problems are outlined below.

Problems to avoid

There are several of these:

Verbosity

The English language, basically logical and easy to understand, lends itself to abuse by the verbose, or wordy, writer. In business communications particularly, never use more words than you need to explain yourself. For example, why say:

'This contract, by its very nature, the subject matter requiring great attention to detail and utilising significant manpower services, will not be ready for completion by the date previously agreed by both parties.'

It would be far clearer and simpler to say:

'Because this contract is very complicated and several people need to work on it, it will not be ready for signature by the date we agreed.'

Clutter

We want to say too much and clutter our sentences with too many ideas. To increase the number of thoughts and the length of the sentence can take the text beyond the level of understanding of the average reader. Complicated construction of sentences makes it impossible for the reader to grasp their meaning without going over them several times. For example:

'The demolition of the old school building at 967 High Street, which has stood empty for years and is now occupied by students who have already protested against the order for their eviction, will go ahead on the 1st March after having been on the schedule of the local authority's Planning Department for some time.'

Far better to break it up thus:

'The old school building at 967 High Street will finally be demolished, after considerable delay. This delay was due to the occupation of the building by students, who are protesting against an eviction order. Until this occupation, the building was empty for many years.'

Repetition

It is best not to repeat a statement, unless it is a deliberate repetition for emphasis, in which case you would say, for example: 'Let me repeat – this order must be completed on time.'

Similarly, try to avoid alliteration – the use of the same sound at the beginning of two or more words. This adds effect to speeches but not to letters. 'The menacing march of progress proceeds at precipitous pace' is rather overdoing it in a letter.

Points to consider

There are several things you should consider for each subject in a communication, as well as the necessity of the document as a whole.

Relevance

We tend not to separate the important from the trivial, which can cause confusion over the priority and validity of the subjects discussed in the communication. It comes back to planning the subject of your letter: only with some preparation will you formulate clear ideas and discard comments that have no particular relevance.

Level of detail

Give your reader all necessary information; never assume that they already possess all the information upon which you may be basing your decision. Always explain background to your letter, without being too wordy. For example:

'As you are probably aware, our company manufactures textiles for export to Eastern Europe. We have built up a considerable market in this part of the world and our machinery, therefore, is geared for mass production of low-cost waterproof material. For us to take on a contract of the size and nature you require would mean a great deal of re-investment in machinery. This would, naturally, push up the price of your textiles and, therefore, we must regretfully decline your business at this stage.'

Necessity

Do not write when it is not necessary. This may seem a rather obvious statement but many of us are guilty of writing unnecessary letters. If you are asked to acknowledge a communication then do so; if a communication you have received obviously requires an answer, then fine, go ahead. Otherwise, don't waste time and paper.

State your purpose

Think about what you really want to say before you write it. Do not write a letter that could be ambiguous. If you want to complain then complain; do not leave the recipient with the feeling that you are not really upset about his or her transgression but just want to moan. This kind of clarity is particularly important for letters relating to the field of employment. Official letters of warning to an employee must be absolutely clear in their intent as they may be shown to a tribunal at a later date if there is any dispute about an eventual dismissal.

Be concise

Present only the essential: it is possible to be polite and brief. For example:

'Thank you for your application for the position of Office Manager. However, the position has been filled by an internal applicant. We wish you luck in any other applications you may make to other companies.'

In such a letter it is not necessary to go into detail about your company's employment policies or the applicant's qualifications – much as he or she would like to know why they failed in their bid for the job. Nowadays, sadly, it is rather gratifying to get a polite rejection: many companies do not even bother to acknowledge receipt of applications.

Use appropriate vocabulary

Vocabulary is all-important. Get it wrong and your letter may be misunderstood or completely baffling to the reader. To ensure successful communication, you need to know which words to use, and which to avoid.

Words to use

Familiar words

These are, generally, the words learnt and known to everybody. These can include technical terms if you are writing to someone who is in your own industry, but don't use written communications to show off your extensive vocabulary. Here are some examples of words that are pretentious and should be avoided:

Pretentious word	*Simple alternative*
ameliorate	make better, or improve
bereft	deprived
coruscate	sparkle
mendacious	lying
veracious	truthful

A more extensive list of pretentious words and their alternatives is provided in the appendix *Troublesome words and phrases* at the back of this book.

Short words

Short expressions are more common than long ones and are less pretentious. For example:

Instead of...	*Use...*
motor car	car
veracity	truth
verbal intercourse	speech
ill-conditioned	bad

Some examples of these are also listed in the appendix *Troublesome words and phrases* at the back of this book.

Words to avoid

Foreign words

Foreign words are superfluous where an English equivalent exists. They should only be used if they are commonly understood and impart a meaning which cannot be easily translated into English. For example 'vice versa' is acceptable, but 'versus' can usually be replaced with 'against' except when describing sports fixtures or legal cases.

Ambiguous words

You must use words that convey exactly what you want to say. Don't leave the reader in any doubt. For example:

'We are uncertain that this course of action will lead to any benefits for the company'.

This suggests to the reader that you are open to persuasion. If you do not wish to be persuaded then say so:

'We do not believe that this course of action is suitable for our company and therefore do not intend to pursue it any further'.

This indicates that your decision is final; no comeback is required or desired.

Redundant words

A clearer and more economical style is obtained by eliminating words that are not doing specific jobs or ones that duplicate a meaning. If you remove the italicised words in the following examples, everything is more direct and uncluttered:

We *first* began the discussion
Very unique
At 5pm *in the afternoon*
Hot *in temperature*

Vogue words

Vogue words, or words that are currently in fashion, do not last and can confuse. Remember, you may not be writing to someone of the same generation, who may therefore not understand you. For example, the following may not mean anything to a reader unfamiliar with hip words:

'We think that your design for the front elevation is really cool.'

'This is a wicked product.'

Incorrect use of words

There are several words that are often used incorrectly, where the writer believes the word to mean something other than its actual meaning. For example, 'effect' and 'affect', or 'practical' and 'practicable'. In the the appendix *Troublesome words and phrases* at the end of this book are several lists of such words; it is recommended that you read and learn these, or at least refer to them before using one of these words to ensure your meaning is clear.

Use correct grammar and punctuation

If a business letter cannot be understood because it is poorly written in terms of grammar, or contains random punctuation, it may well not achieve its purpose. The recipient of your letter may spend so much effort in trying to sort out exactly what you mean, he or she may forget the important point that you had just made or may lose track of the overall argument. So it is in order to avoid confusion and misunderstanding, as well as to give a good impression of yourself and your business, that you should try to write and punctuate correctly.

Unfortunately for the average letter writer, language is a living entity and correct usage changes over the years. Furthermore, constructions which are permissible in daily conversation may not be grammatically acceptable in writing prose. The gap between what is allowable in speech and what is correct in writing presents considerable difficulty to many people. The rules of English grammar are extremely complicated but for the purposes of business letter writing it is sufficient to be familiar with the basic structure of a correct sentence and the rules of proper punctuation. If you know those and avoid trying to write long and complex sentences, you should avoid many mistakes. Keep a dictionary beside you to check any spellings of which you are unsure, and be aware of the common pitfalls listed in this section.

Use proper sentences

It is of the utmost importance, for the sake of readability and understanding, that you use clearly laid-out sentences. The reader will find long complex sentences and those that do not convey an instantly clear message difficult to digest.

Read these examples and judge for yourself:

'The man who presents the reasons for the delay in implementing the necessary job-destroying investments planned for October, which should also save costs and guarantee the continuing market share for product X, encounters little understanding.'

or alternatively:

'There are plans for investment in October. These will destroy jobs but should also reduce costs and retain the market share product X presently enjoys. Whoever has to present the reasons for the delay in this investment will encounter little sympathy.'

The first example is a very long sentence, shrouded in complexity. By contrast, the second example presents the same information in three short, clear sentences.

If you consider it important to be understood, then the construction of your sentences should not present your listeners with a brain teaser. If you want to inform and convince, you have to make it easy for your reader to comprehend your thoughts. Grammatical finesse and rhetorical beauty are thus not always required. To make your letter understandable the language should really serve as a means to an end.

What exactly is a sentence?

This may sound a simple question, but it is not always obvious.

A sentence is defined as a group of words that makes complete sense on its own. In order to do this it must contain two parts: the subject, a word or words about which the sentence will say something, and a predicate, a word or words about the subject. For example, in the sentence

'The conference is postponed'

The first part, 'The conference', is the subject, and the second part, 'is postponed', is the predicate.

Guidelines for writing sentences

Note the following guidelines when writing a sentence:

- Avoid splitting the subject and predicate.
  OK: 'After arguing the point in the meeting, David consented to allow it.'
  Not OK: 'David, after arguing the point in the meeting, consented to allow it.'

- Avoid splitting an infinitive (to call, to meet, to do).
  OK: 'Peter wanted to check each order carefully and meticulously.'
  Not OK: 'Peter wanted to carefully and meticulously check each order.'

- Keep the same subject.
  OK: 'We were hungry at the conference because we forgot to order lunch.'
  Not OK: 'We were hungry at the conference because one forgot to order lunch.'

- Keep the same tense.
  OK: 'Jane answered the telephone but nobody spoke.'
  Not OK: 'Jane answered the telephone but nobody speaks.'

Following are some rules for the clear, easy-to-comprehend formulation of sentences.

Use short sentences
Construct short, uncomplicated sentences. As a simple rule of thumb – new idea, new sentence.

Limit subordinate clauses
For each main clause or idea, use only one subordinate clause. Accumulating subordinate clauses leads to a forest of words which the reader has to hack through, frequently having to backtrack to grasp the main point that is being made. Look at the following example of a sentence with several subordinate clauses (they are all italicised):

'It is important that any employee who saw the man who stole a car from the staff car park, *reports state that he was dark-haired, other reports state that he was wearing a blue bomber jacket, and yet another report states that he was about twenty-five years old,* should come and see the personnel officer immediately, *providing that they are not interrupting their work or that the personnel officer is available.'*

It would be better to say :

'Would any employee who saw the man who stole a car from the staff car park please visit the personnel officer immediately. Please check first that the personnel officer is available, and do not interrupt your work. We have received various reports that the man was about twenty-five years of age, dark-haired and wearing a blue bomber jacket.'

Some grammatical pitfalls

There are several areas of grammar that trip up even the most experienced of writers. Here are some tips for how to avoid them.

Collective nouns

Collective nouns are nouns that are singular in form but refer to a group of persons or things. One must be careful to use a singular or a plural verb depending upon the purpose of the particular sentence. For example:

'The committee was furious with the plans for a strike.'

This is singular because the committee was acting as a group.

'The committee were arguing among themselves over the plans for a strike.'

In this case, the committee were obviously acting as individuals, not as a unit.

Pronouns

The most common error involving pronouns is in phrases using 'me', 'myself' and 'I'. For example, 'between you and I' should be 'between you and me'. The best way to get this right is to imagine the other person is removed: it would make no sense to say 'That was written by I' or 'That was written by myself'; you would say 'That was written by me'. Therefore, it cannot be correct to say 'That was written by Mary and I' or 'That was written by Mary and myself'; rather 'That was written by Mary and me' is correct.

Adjectives

Similar to the problem of the collective noun is the problem of 'distributive' adjectives and pronouns. These include: anybody, nobody, everybody, either, neither, each, every, none. They are all singular and must be used with verbs and pronouns in the singular. For example:

OK: 'Everybody who travels abroad must have his or her passport.'

Not OK: 'Everybody who travels abroad must have their passport.'

OK: 'Each of the staff was given a certificate after the course.'

Not OK: 'Each of the staff were given a certificate after the course.'

There is a tendency to use 'they' and 'their' to work around the problem of language being considered sexist. Indeed, many would say that the second version of the passports example is correct in the sense that it does not discriminate. The alternative forms 's/he' or 'his/her' are clumsy and unattractive, but there is usually another way around the situation, even if it means reversing the order of the sentence or stating both pronouns, as in the correct version above.

Verbs

Verbs are singular or plural depending on the singular or plural nature of their subject.

For example, the following are both correct:

'Those plates, left from the managers' meeting, have not been washed.'

'That stack of plates, left from the managers' meeting, has not been washed.'

because in the first example the plates are the subject, while in the second the stack is the subject.

The use of 'and' is like the plus sign in mathematics and makes a plural total.

'John and Kathy were in the canteen.'

If we use any other words to join John and Kathy, this does not happen.

'John, as well as his colleague Kathy, was in the canteen.'

Adverbs

The most common mistake here is to use an adjective when an adverb is required.

OK: 'She read the letters very quickly.'
Not OK: 'She read the letters very quick.'

Prepositions

Avoid using the prepositional phrase 'due to' when ' because of' conveys the correct idea of causation:

OK: 'The company cricket match was stopped because of the rain.'
Not OK: 'The company cricket match was stopped due to the rain.'

Avoid using the verb 'following' when prepositions and prepositional phrases such as 'after', 'because of', 'as a result of', and 'in accordance with' are more accurate.

OK: 'Because of the heavy rain the car park flooded.'
Not OK: 'Following the heavy rain the car park flooded.'

Miscellaneous errors

Than

The word 'than' causes a lot of confusion when followed by a personal pronoun. For example:
'John is cleverer than me.'

This is incorrect because the complete sentence would be:
'John is cleverer than I am.'
Therefore you should write
'John is cleverer than I.'
(See *Pronouns* for further discussion of the use of 'I', 'me', and 'myself'.)

Less and fewer

'Fewer' should be used when the persons or object referred to can be counted; 'less' when what is referred to cannot be counted. For example:

'James ate no fewer than four biscuits at tea.'

'James takes less sugar in his tea than I do.'

The exception to this rule is for statements about time and distance. For example:

'London is less than 32 kilometres from our office; it takes less than an hour to get there.'

Use proper punctuation

The most commonly used punctuation marks in English are:

Full stop	.
Colon	:
Semicolon	;
Comma	,
Parentheses	( )
Dash	–
Question mark	?
Exclamation mark	!
Quotation marks	''
Apostrophe	'

While most of us will recognise most, if not all, of these, they are very often misused in even the most professional-looking documents. Aim higher than this and make sure you use punctuation correctly and to the best effect.

Full stop

Every declarative sentence must end with a full stop.

Colon

The colon signals that an explanation or further information follows. It is often used to introduce a series, for example:

'The accounts manager wants three things from you: a timesheet, your holiday request, and your tax code'.

It is also used to introduce a quotation:

'My manager's favourite saying is: "An untidy desk is the sign of a genius".'

It is also used to separate two clauses of equal weight:

'Paul said it was time for the meeting: I said we had just finished discussing the agenda'.

Semicolon

This functions mainly in a long sentence to separate clauses where a pause between a comma and a full stop is needed.

Comma

The comma is the most frequently used punctuation mark. It is used to separate items in a list of three or more words, as in the example for colons shown earlier.

It is also used to separate phrases which depend on the same word:

'I have worked in Canada for a stockbroker, in Egypt for a travel agent, and in England for an accountant'.

It can also be used in a long sentence where a natural pause occurs.

Parentheses

These are sometimes known as brackets, although strictly speaking a bracket is the square version like this [ ].

Use parentheses in pairs when an interruption or aside is not necessarily relevant to the main idea of the sentence.

Dash

A pair of dashes may be used to replace parentheses; a single dash may be used in informal contexts to replace the colon. Dashes should not be used as all-purpose punctuation marks.

Question mark

This is used at the end of a sentence which is a direct question, such as:

'Is there any paper in the printer?'

Do not use for indirect questions, such as:

'Mr Jones asked whether there was any paper in the printer.'

Exclamation mark

This is used at the end of a sentence when a strong feeling is present. A single exclamation mark is enough. Generally exclamation marks are over-used and are unnecessary in most business documents, although they are often found in promotional material.

Quotation marks

These are used in pairs to enclose direct quotations, for example:

'He asked "Where is my secretary?" and called her name.'

Full stops and commas go inside the quotation marks when they directly relate to the matter quoted.

Use single quotes for examples, as used in this book.

Apostrophe

This is used as a mark of omission as in won't, can't or it's (sometimes known as contraction or elision), but such forms are rarely used in business documents – instead, spell the words out in full. For example:

OK: 'I will not be able to meet you on Tuesday.'
Not OK: 'I won't be able to meet you on Tuesday.'

The apostrophe is also used to show possession, either singular or plural, for example:

'This is Mary's printer.' (singular)

'Where are the receptionist's keys?' (singular)

'Where are the receptionists' keys?' (plural, indicating more than one receptionist).

When to use capital letters

Use an initial capital letter for the following situations only:

- To begin a new sentence
- To mark a proper noun or adjective (England, Englishman)
- To write the days of the week and the months of the year
- To begin a full quotation
- To write the names of companies, books, films, newspapers
- To name specific courses (GCSE, NVQ).

Do not use a capital letter for subject names or for seasons.

Do not use block capitals in general text (they may be used for certain parts of a letter, as indicated previously) as they are difficult to read and are associated with heavy emphasis.

Use correct spelling

It is of utmost importance that you spell words accurately in a business document. It is possible to mislead or misinform through the casual or incorrect use of similar-sounding words, and sloppy spelling indicates a non-professional attitude.

A list of words that are commonly confused or misspelled is provided in the appendix *Troublesome words and phrases* at the end of this book; meanwhile, here are a few tips on successful spelling.

Checking your spelling

When you are unsure of a spelling, look it up in a dictionary – either book or computer. Beware of computer spell-checkers however; they will only identify a word as being wrong if it does not appear in their dictionary: for example, if you type 'through' instead of 'thorough' or 'on' instead of 'in', the computer will not pick this up as an error.

Rules and their exceptions

Spelling is governed by rules, most of which, to be difficult, have a few exceptions. Those that seem to cause the most problems are described below.

I before e...

A simple rhyme to remember when spelling words with 'ie' or 'ei' is:

I before E
Except after C
Or when sounded as A
As in neighbour or weigh.

Adding prefixes and suffixes

A prefix is one or more letters or syllables added onto the beginning of a root word. When a prefix is added, the spelling of the root word remains unchanged.

Dis + appear = disappear

Over + worked = overworked

A suffix is one or more letters or syllables added to the end of a root word. Rules to remember when adding suffixes are:

- A silent 'e' is normally dropped before adding the suffix, for example:
  Bore + ing = boring
  Change + ed = changed.
- Don't drop the 'e' for words ending in 'ce' or 'ge' where the suffix starts with a consonant, for example:
  Encourage + ment = encouragement
  Sage + ly = sagely
  but continue to drop it when the suffix starts with a vowel:
  Coerce + ion = coercion
  Garage + ed = garaged
- Add a 'k' to words ending in c, for example:
  Picnic + ing becomes picnicking
  Panic + ed becomes panicked.

General guidelines for writing

Everyone has their own style and so it would be foolish to lay down rules that might destroy the individuality that lies behind the way people write. However, the following points will help you to get the right emphasis at certain points of your letter and develop some style.

State your point early

The main statement is the main clause and should come at the beginning of the sentence. The longer the reader has to wait for the main clause, or the point of the sentence, the greater the danger they will lose the thread and be unable to identify the meaning correctly.

Express yourself precisely

Wherever possible, use expressions that are short and precise; don't stretch them out. For example:

Wordy expression	*Short, precise alternative*
would seem to imply	implies
this moment in time	now
for that reason	because
in recent times	recently

A more extensive list of wordy expressions, clichés and their alternatives is provided in the reference section at the back of this book.

Avoid humour

Do not try to use irony or humour in a business letter, as this is easily misunderstood. Irony particularly needs the human voice and face to tell the other person you are being ironic. For example, how would you take the following?

'That will really please him.'

In print, it comes across as a sincere statement. However, what was really meant was:

'I don't think he'll be pleased about that at all!'

It is possible in some communication formats to hint at the true meaning through the use of emphasis (bold or italic for example). However, this doesn't always work. Would it really make the meaning any clearer to italicise the word 'really' in the first example?

Make it natural

Probably the most effective advice that anyone can give about the use of English in written communications is to make it as natural as your thought processes. If your thought processes are a little muddled, return to the planning stage again. Make some notes for yourself to keep you on the right track. If you are unsure about the flow of a letter, or where to punctuate, read it out aloud: punctuation should occur where you feel you have to take a small breath or change emphasis or idea.

Further information

There are many publications that offer advice on grammar, punctuation and style. Whether you need to use them will depend on your confidence in your written English, as well as the types of document you are writing. For most letter-writing, a good-quality dictionary will be sufficient; if writing on technical subjects, try to obtain a dictionary specific to those subjects. Other guides to grammar and usage of English, such as the widely used *Fowler's Guide to Modern English Usage* (Oxford University Press), are useful for larger projects and contain extended information on some of the grammar issues discussed in this chapter.

CHAPTER 4

International correspondence

In this chapter we look at issues specific to international correspondence: how to make the initial approach to an overseas reader, when to use your own language and when to use theirs; and how to choose and use translation services.

The first contact

Doing business abroad often begins with a letter, fax or e-mail, although many in the export business say that you cannot beat face-to-face contact. Certainly there are some countries whose culture demands that business be generated by personal contact: many South American companies, for example, like the first approach to be face-to-face because they like to see the man or woman who wishes to do business with them. However, some nationalities prefer to start business negotiations in writing: Belgians and Scandinavians, for example, love to show how adept they are at several languages, particularly English.

Which language to use

It has been accepted in recent years that English is the language of international business. In fact more business communities in the world speak Chinese, Russian or Spanish than English as their first language, but English has become acceptable to all, probably because it tends to be the second language of most of these countries. It may also be partly due to the rise in the importance of computers in business, and the domination of the computer industry by American companies: although most business software is nowadays available in a variety of languages, this is a relatively recent development.

Nevertheless, it is generally considered a courtesy to make the first written approach to an overseas company in their language wherever possible. If they respond in English, you can conduct future business in the language that they have chosen. The sensible thing to do is to write a good letter of approach, have it translated into the necessary language and make sure that the recipient is aware that you have had it translated, so that they know that you, personally, are not fluent in their language. If they cannot respond in English then they will also use a translator.

We will look at how to obtain a translator, and what to look for, later in this chapter.

Which layout to use

Another reason for consulting an expert is that some countries use different styles or layouts for letters and other business correspondence, and it gives a good impression if you copy that style where possible. Although it would rarely cause offence if you stuck to your usual letter layout, it is a welcome gesture which proves the serious intent of your communication. For example, the following layouts are used as standard in the countries from which they originate: Equatorial Guinea (Figure 9) and Germany (Figure 10).

Republica de Guinea Ecuatorial
Ministeria De …

Núm. 2000.E08-050
Ref. -
Sccc. -

Malabo, 3 de Encro de 2000

Att: General Gordon
Director
MAJOR PETROLEUM PLC
London UK
Fax : (44 171) 999 2020

Estimado Generalissimo Gordon:
(main body of text)

No obstante, y mientras tanto, los descamos un feliz y próspero año nuevo.

Sin otro etc...

Figure 9: An international letter format

Note how the references and filing details are aligned to the left of the page, the date to the right. Also, the manner of laying out the recipient's address is quite unusual. The salutation 'Estimado Generalissimo Gordon' means 'Most dear (or Esteemed) General Gordon'; the complimentary close 'Sin otro' literally 'Without others', or 'Yours alone'.

Now let's look at the German format.

B.J.MANN & SOHN
Import- Export
Hamburg
Mullerstrasse 9

Herren Schmidt & Hausen
Heidenheim a.d.Brenz
Haupstrasse 20

16. October 1999

Ihre Zeichen/Nachricht	Unsere Zeichen/Nachricht	Betreff
M/F 8.9.1999	H/P	Steingut-Krüge

Auf Grund Ihres Angebots vom 4. September dieses Jahres...
(main body of text)
Hochachtungsvoll

B.J.Mann & Sohn

Figure 10: Another international letter format

In this letter, the preferred style is to range all the references across the top of the letter: 'Ihre Zeichen/Ihre Nachricht' meaning 'Your ref/date', 'Unsere Zeichen/Nachricht' meaning 'Our ref/date' and 'Betreff' meaning 'Reference or Re:', the subject matter of the letter. Note that there is no salutation at the beginning of the letter. The complimentary close 'Hochachtungsvoll' means 'Respectfully'.

Using translation services

Here we look at the use of translation services; what to look for in a translator and whether machine or computerised translation can be a suitable alternative.

Choosing a translator

When choosing a translation company there are several points to consider:

- Do you need a translator with specific technical skills? For example, if you need to translate medical, engineering or scientific terms, you may need someone with the appropriate experience.
- Are you translating into a European language or an Oriental language? What is the final destination? Some translation companies specialise in the various languages and dialects of particular countries or regions; remember that, for example, Portuguese is spoken and written quite differently in Portugal than in certain areas of South America.
- If you have someone in-house who can draft basic letters adequately in the required language, will the translator just check them over for a modest fee?
- Is the translator or translation company reputable? Do they use fully qualified linguists? Embassies are a good place to start if you want to find a translation company that will do a good job, or if you have special requirements: the commercial attachés often know of translators with a good reputation for translating their own language.

Do's and don'ts

In addition here are a few do's and don'ts, compiled from the recommendations of several professional translators, translation companies and their clients:

- DO assess your needs before you approach a translator. Know what language you require, and whether you require only the letter to be translated, or other supporting documentation as well (such as brochures).

- DO make sure the translator is experienced in using the required software, if you want the work completed on-screen (for example, you may want them to type their translation into Microsoft Word or Claris Works). This is particularly important for more complex documents such as printed brochures.
- DO use a professional, qualified translator who specialises in the required language. An all-rounder may not have the required knowledge to produce professional business documents. When using a translation company or agency, always request details of the qualifications of the particular translator who will be handling the work. Ask for references and check credentials. Remember that you will be unable to assess the quality of the translation if you do not understand the language yourself, so make as certain as possible that the quality will be good.
- DO select a translator who is a member of a reputable professional organisation (some are listed at the end of this chapter). Such bodies offer reassurance of the quality of the translator's work, and a point of reference in case of any problems. Most have entry criteria or require members to undergo qualification tests. There is no official accreditation system for translators in the UK, but there are in many other countries, so if you are looking for translators abroad, ask for accreditation details.
- DO acknowledge the translator or translation company in the translated document (see *Acknowledging the use of a translator* overleaf).
- DON'T select a translator simply on the basis of cost. Remember that the best qualified person in any industry is usually the highest paid. Your business is too important to lose through an inadequate, but cheap, translation.
- DON'T ask a translator to translate a sample for free. While you are fully entitled to see samples of previous work, most translators work for low margins and simply cannot afford the time to offer free sample translations. Any that do will compensate by upping their charges on the paid work.

- DON'T assume that local is best. There is a general courtesy agreement between translators that they only handle work written in the native language of the country they work in. For example, to translate from German to English one would generally seek a translator in Germany, whereas from English to German one would ask a UK-based translator. Most translation agencies and companies have partner agencies abroad with whom they exchange work, so it is usually possible to avoid the need to search internationally for the service you require. These days, of course, it is also possible to source translation services via the Internet, but always check the credentials, wherever the source.
- DON'T send confidential material requiring translation via e-mail or the Internet. Use a more secure method.

There are additional items to consider when using computerised translation; these are listed later, in the section *Computerised translation*.

Acknowledging the use of a translator

Do not feel embarrassed at your lack of language skills and hide the fact that you have used a translator. It is common practice in international business, and can help to foster trust in your overseas client. For example, it is particularly important when dealing with Far Eastern companies that they do not lose face by being made to feel inadequate. If they feel that you are fluent in their language but they are not fluent in yours, it will put them in an inferior position and they will not respond to your letter through embarrassment. If they know that you have had to use a translator then they will feel better and are more likely to do the same.

American companies, who are very experienced at doing business in the Far East, often put a postscript at the bottom of their letters stating that the letter was translated by such and such a company. Others may choose to mention it in the main text.

There is another good reason for mentioning in your letter that it has been translated by a specialist translator. If the translation is not very good, the recipient will feel free to mention that fact and you will be able to take the appropriate action. After all, if you do not speak their language, you have no way of checking whether the translator has done a good job. If you are passing off the translation as your own, the recipient might feel too embarrassed to tell you that it is awful.

Translation of official or legal documents

This is an area that requires an expert. Many legal documents, such as those issued by a Registrar, must be officially 'sworn' after translation to ensure they are valid; others may simply require a declaration by the translator on separate, headed paper to establish their correctness. Documents for official use in the UK or EU require a declaration before a solicitor; for use outside the EU the declaration must be made before a Notary Public. These services are expensive, and may sometimes be avoided through the use of the destination country's embassy and one of their sworn translators. Contact the embassy for further information.

Computerised translation

Machine translation and translation memory software offer an alternative to the human translator. But is it a viable alternative?

The limitations

Automated translation facilities have been available since the 1960s. When you consider the massive advances in general computerised technology since that time, it is surprising how little progress has been made in this area. Certainly until recently, computer translations had a very bad name, not only among professional translators (for obvious reasons) but also among the persons on whom such translations were inflicted. While computerised translation is certainly suitable for some tasks, notably where standard phrases are used such as in share listings, certain catalogues and, notably, weather forecasts, it is certainly not the answer for all business correspondence.

Here are some arguments for and against:

For	*Against*
Allows quick basic translation of large documents	Can only be used if the source text is in electronic form (a computer file)

Dictionary functions useful as an aid to the human translator	Requires large amounts of computer memory to hold its word banks, which often contain in excess of 100,000 words
May offer more than one language (some products)	Expensive to buy, especially if many languages are required
Can update dictionaries from a central website (some products only)	May not provide an accurate translation of words with more than one meaning
May allow voice-activated translation and interpretation (some products)	Requires the original text to contain perfect use of grammar, punctuation and vocabulary
Can translate incoming foreign e-mail (some products)	

Getting the best from computerised translation

The following tips for getting the best from machine translation are provided by a major manufacturer of translation software.

People's expectation of machine translation can sometimes be rather high. The software can do a good job, but it requires more thought on the part of the user than some people imagine: remember that machines do not have the reasoning capabilities of humans. Therefore, in order to obtain the best results from machine translation, documents must be written in clear, concise, proper English.

Producing good machine translation text is identical to producing text that humans can read easily without extra effort. Here are some tips.

Write in standard, formal English

In formal English, grammatical connections are clearly expressed: subjects agree with predicates, modifiers relate to what they modify. Unnecessary words are kept to a minimum. Clear formal writing, which is easiest for your reader to understand, will result in the most comprehensible translations possible. Informal English is marked by loose grammatical style that is typical of everyday speech. This may be perfectly appropriate for conversation, but it is not beneficial for the translation process.

Write clearly and explicitly

Machines cannot read between the lines. They only translate what is there, not what the author might have intended. The more straightforward the information in the sentences, the better translation you will receive. Avoid ambiguity, unclear references, colloquialisms and slang. Use consistent names for objects.

Proofread before you translate

Always ensure that the typed text is 100% accurate. Pay particular attention to spelling and punctuation.

Check the layout of the document

When writing the original document, allow text to wrap naturally as hard returns are interpreted as line breaks, implying the end of a sentence. Make heading information explicit as headings often contain different grammar conventions than normal text; for example, they may use initial or full capitals. Ensure each point in a bulleted or numbered list is grammatically well formed or the machine may try to reconstruct a complete sentence.

Avoid idiomatic expressions

If you are not sure whether a phrase is an idiom, consider the literal meaning of the words. If the literal sense is not clear, try to express the same idea in a different way. For example:

OK: It rarely happens.
Not OK: It happens once in a blue moon.

Use proper grammar

Use a pronoun before a verb, even if it can be implied and the sentence is understandable without it.

OK: I studied history but I did not learn much.
Not OK: I studied history but did not learn much.

Do not omit words

Words like 'that', 'which', 'who' and 'whom' are often implied in English but are required in other languages.

OK: I know that Bob works on Monday.
Not OK: I know Bob works on Monday.

Use possessive apostrophes only

Use apostrophes to indicate possession, but not to indicate contraction of words.

OK: Mary is singing at the church tonight.
Not OK: Mary's singing at the church tonight.
Also OK: Mary's singing at the church tonight was wonderful.

(In this case the apostrophe indicates possession – the singing was done by Mary.)

Use simple, clear sentences

Keep your sentence structure clear, simple and direct. Break up long sentences of many ideas into short sentences expressing one main idea. For example:

OK: The local government completed projects including the construction of a bridge. This bridge allows travel between our city and Springfield. It has increased commerce in both communities.
Not OK: The local government completed projects including the construction of a new bridge, which allows travel between our city and Springfield and has increased commerce in both communities.

Do not split verbs

Do not separate compound English verbs, such as 'pick up' and 'look up'. Although acceptable in speech, it could cause translation errors. Avoid these verbs if there is an alternative.

OK: I have to look up the information in our database.
Not OK: I have to look the information up in our database.

Use accents correctly

When possible, enter text with the correct diacritical marks. Some accent marks look very similar but misuse may lead to an incorrect translation.

Update the dictionary

Machines can only translate words that are in its lexicon, as these are the only words the machine knows. An unknown word can lead to a misinterpretation of the complete sentence. Most machine translation systems today allow you to add unknown words to the dictionary before translating the document, increasing the accuracy of the final translation.

Check context when translating interactively

When using an interactive translation feature, you will be prompted to choose between multiple translations. Use the surrounding text to aid in your decision-making. With some products, the first draft of such interactive translation is solely to select the correct vocabulary: all words appear in their root forms without appropriate conjugation.

The future of machine translation

It is now possible to obtain a mixture of machine translation and human translation on the Internet. Certain ISPs and websites offer free machine translation of small documents, with the option to refer the document to a human translator for checking (for which a fee is required). Such systems have not yet been available for long enough for a reasoned judgement to be made on their effectiveness when compared with the more traditional translation options.

Certain machine translation providers allow large companies to link directly to their Intranet to take advantage of all the available language options without requiring large, expensive computers and many different software packages. This is useful if your company requires documents in diverse languages, but offers no other advantage over standard machine translation, although the companies who offer such schemes predict it to be the translation route of the future.

Finally it may be useful to note that, despite all this, some of the largest producers of translation software continue to employ human translators to translate some corporate documents, even simple documents that their software could probably handle with ease!

CHAPTER 5

Technology for communication

In this chapter, we look at the ways in which computers and their software can assist with business communication; how to best use them according to your experience to create professional-looking letters, faxes and memos; and what part e-mail can play in business communication.

How computer software can help with communication

Today, most computers designed for home and office, whether PC or Macintosh, are supplied with software for word-processing already installed. Such software often contains templates for writing letters and other forms of business communications, allowing you to quickly and easily construct attractive-looking documents. The software may also offer secretarial functions such as automatic text correction, spell-checking, automatic insertion of standard phrases and so on. While you may initially have a few problems understanding how such functions work and be tempted to compose your letters in the old-fashioned way for the sake of speed, with a little practice and reference to the manual or online help you will be able to make the software do what you want, to produce high-quality documents with ease.

Much of this software is developed by large American corporations, and until recently the tendency to use American formats for dates, spellings, and even paper sizes was a problem for non-US users. This is now less common, and most new computers sold with pre-installed software are 'localised' to contain the language version appropriate to the country in which they are sold. If your existing software does use American spellings, check whether a more suitable dictionary is supplied: it is normally known as British English, or UK English. You may need to change this setting for several applications, including the operating system, to get the full benefit: ask your computer retailer or the manufacturer for details if you cannot find the information you require in the manuals.

Recently, word-processing software has been improved to make it easier for the novice to use. For example, many of Microsoft's products offer 'wizards', which guide you through creating a particular type of document; auto-correction, which learns from your mistakes to correct words you commonly misspell; and autotext, which tries to anticipate what you are typing and pops up suggested text on the screen for you to select if you don't want to type the word out in full. Other software manufacturers offer similarly useful aids, usually with different names. Experienced users often complain about the 'intrusion' of these features, but they are useful to a beginner, and you can always switch them off if they irritate you. Other features, such as grammar and spell-checkers, are useful but it must be remembered that they are not infallible: if you type 'though' in place of 'through', for example, neither the spell-checker nor the grammar checker will recognise it as an error, but your sentence will not make sense. Nothing replaces the human eye as an efficient proofreader.

How to create a business document

How you go about creating a letter or other business document with your word-processing or desktop publishing (DTP) software depends on the following:

- Which software you are using: while they are all fairly similar, some products have functions the others do not
- How experienced you are with the use of computers, and with similar software
- What type of document you are creating
- If a letter, whether you use headed notepaper.

In this book, we use examples from Microsoft Word, a product widely used by business. Most of the examples could be created equally well with another word-processor, or with a suitable DTP product.

Automatic formatting

The letter shown below was created using Microsoft Word. The text was typed in a basic fashion and the AutoFormat facility selected. This automatically rearranged the letter into the correct letter format you see here. As it is intended to be printed onto letterheaded paper, no sender's address was included.

John Smith
The Old Mill Company
River Stream
DROITWICH
D99 7BB

25 February 2000
Your Ref OP/98
Dear Mr Smith,
Re: New carriage for the Mayor

Please find enclosed our specifications for a new carriage to be built for the Mayor of Minetown. We hope that you will be able to meet these specifications and the deadline for completion as discussed at our meeting.
As soon as we receive your written confirmation of this we will issue a contract.

Yours sincerely,

Mr Peter Potts
Co-ordinator
The Lord Mayor's Office

Figure 11: An automatically formatted letter

Wizards

If you are not familiar with your software, you may find wizards a useful way to learn. These are basically a series of prompts that guide you through the process of creating a particular type of document. For example, when the wizards option is switched on, if you start typing a letter a message will appear saying 'It looks as though you are typing a letter' and offering the use of the Letter Wizard. If you agree, you are presented with a series of screens that you must complete – rather similar to filling in an on-screen form. You must type certain parts of the letter such as the name and address of the recipient and sender, while other parts, such as the salutation, can be added automatically according to which style you select (for example, formal style would use the salutation 'Dear Sirs'). This produces a professional-looking letter format on screen and all you have to do is fill in the main body of the letter.

Templates

Whatever document you create, and whatever your experience, you will probably use a template (some products may call it something else). For letters, if your notepaper is headed, you will probably just use a 'blank document' template, leaving space at the top of the page to compensate for the pre-printed area. However, there are a variety of other templates designed for those without a letterheading, and these create everything for you including graphics and layout: all you have to do is type in the relevant details where indicated. Templates are also available for faxes, memos and other documents. Some examples of templates supplied with Microsoft Word are shown below.

Company Name Here
3 March, 2000

[Click here and type recipient's address]

Dear Sir or Madam:

Type your letter here. For more details on modifying this letter template, double-click . To return to this letter, use the Window menu.

Sincerely,

[Click here and type your name]
[Click here and type job title]

Figure 12: Microsoft Word Contemporary Letter 1 template

facsimile transmittal sheet	
to:	from:
[Click here and type name]	[Click here and type name]
company:	date:
[Click here and type name]	3 March, 2000
fax number:	total no. of pages including
cover: [Click here and type fax number]	[Click here and type number of pages]
Phone number:	sender's reference number:
[Click here and type phone number]	[Click here and type reference number]
Re:	Your reference number:
[Click here and type subject of fax]	[Click here and type reference number]

❑ Urgent ❑ For Revise ❑ Please Comment ❑ Please Reply ❑ Please Recycle

Notes/Comments:

Select this text and delete it or replace it with your own. To save changes to this template for future use, choose Save As from the File menu. In the Save As Type box, choose Document Template. Next time you want to use it, choose New from the File menu, and then double-click your template.

Figure 13: Microsoft Word Professional Fax template

Company Name Here

Memo

To: [click here and type name]

From: [click here and type name]

CC: [click here and type name]

Date: 3 March, 2000

Re: [click here and type subject]

How to Use This Memo Template

Select text you would like to replace, and type your memo. Use styles such as Heading 1-3 and Body Text in the Style control on the Formatting toolbar. To save changes to this template for future use, choose Save As from the File menu. In the Save As Type box, choose Document Template. Next time you want to use it, choose New from the File menu, and then double-click your template.

Figure 14: Microsoft Word Professional Memo template

Mail merge

Many word-processing and DTP applications also offer a facility to merge a list or database of names and addresses with a form letter. This allows you to create a mass mailing of seemingly personalised letters – all individually addressed with each individual greeted by name but with the letter containing standard information. This is particularly useful when you need to send the same letter to a large number of people. Facilities and functions vary considerably from one product to another, so it would not be helpful to try and talk you through the process in this book. You should consult the manual or online help that accompanies your software for details of how to use this function.

Using electronic mail (e-mail)

To send and receive e-mail you need the following:

- A suitable personal computer with a modem, to allow you to send the electronic message files across the telephone network.
- Connection software, which converts your typed message into a format that can be sent via the modem, and also provides you with an e-mail address, storage on a remote server for incoming messages, and access to the Internet. This software is provided by an ISP (Internet Service Provider); some may be pre-installed on your computer.
- E-mail software, to allow you to type and send, receive and read messages, and usually, to file them in a structured way. Again, one or more such applications may be pre-installed if you have a recently purchased computer.

You do not need to necessarily purchase this equipment yourself; see *Using Internet cafés and libraries* later in this chapter.

Modems

Most computers for home and office are supplied with a modem already installed; if not it is easy to purchase one and attach it to your computer. Contact a computer dealer or superstore for details of a suitable product for your computer.

Connection software

Connection software, and the connections it enables, used to be expensive to purchase and operate. Now, many ISPs are giving away the software for free – so anxious are they to get people on to the Internet. You will find this software arriving, unsolicited, through the post and being given away in computer shops and high street newsagents – in fact almost anywhere. If you already have ISP software and are being charged a fee for using it, it is time to change to another supplier. Some companies now also offer free telephone time (without this, you must pay the cost of the telephone call each time you log on to send or receive messages, or use the Internet), and it is expected that this will become the norm, as it is in the United States. Technically, all ISP software offers much the same functionality.

E-mail software

Again, most new computers will have one or more e-mail programs pre-installed, usually Microsoft Outlook Express, Netscape Communicator or CompuServe. You do not have to use these products any more than you have to use a specific ISP; rather choose the one that suits you best. The software makes sending e-mail very simple – the layout of the window into which you type your message may vary but the names of the tasks are fairly standard. If you do have to pay for telephone time, remember to compose your e-mail 'off-line' (without connecting to the phone line). It costs you nothing to write off-line and you can save costs by waiting until you have several messages to send before connecting to the Internet and transmitting your e-mail.

Using Internet cafés and libraries

It is possible to send and receive e-mail even if you do not have a computer of your own. As long as you have regular access to a computer containing the above software in, say, a library or Internet café, you can log on to one of the websites that offer free e-mail addresses. The best known at the time of writing this book are Netaddress (www.netaddress.com), Mailcity (www.mailcity.com) and Hotmail (www.hotmail.com). These allow you to send or receive e-mail by logging on to the Internet, selecting the company's site and typing in your name and password. This works rather like an old-fashioned accommodation address – somewhere you can pick up your mail – except that you don't have to pay. However, there is usually a charge levied by the premises for the use of such facilities, often on an hourly basis, to cover the cost of telephone usage, so if you are using the Internet or e-mail regularly, shop around for the best prices. It is a good way to try out the Internet and e-mail, to see if it is for you, before deciding whether to invest in equipment of your own.

E-mail is discussed more fully in the next chapter, *All about e-mail.*

CHAPTER 6

All about e-mail

In this chapter we look in detail at the use of electronic mail (e-mail) as a business communication, including how it works, how to get started, rules to follow, and when and when not to use it. Details of the equipment you need to use e-mail is given in the previous chapter.

Why is e-mail so popular?

The ability to send e-mail has been the most important part of the development of the Internet. E-mail is cheaper than a telephone call and quicker than a letter, so it is not surprising that the business community has embraced the facility with such relish. E-mail can include words, pictures, sounds and video clips – in fact any kind of computer file – and can be sent to more than one location simultaneously, making it ideal for business communications that require supporting visual or audio material.

The appearance of e-mail depends upon which e-mail software you are using. A typical example is shown overleaf (taken from Microsoft Outlook Express).

The functionality of e-mail

E-mail is regarded as a functional method of communication comprising 'messages', rather than something aesthetically pleasing that can represent the image of your company in the way that a letter on letterheaded paper does. For this reason, there is little scope for making e-mail visually attractive. While many new e-mail applications allow you to write and read text coded in HTML (see the chapter *Structure, layout and style*), and even offer graphical backgrounds, like printed notepaper,

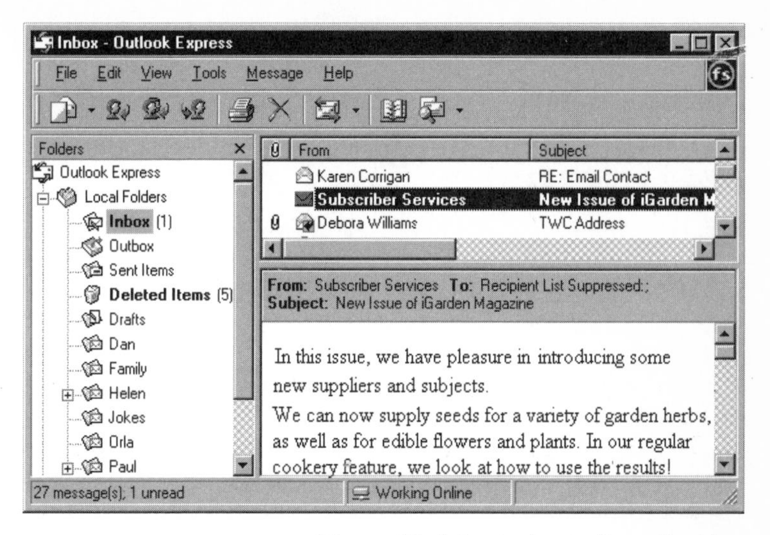

Figure 15: A typical e-mail application

on which you can type your message, these are not yet in standard use, and users of different e-mail software may be unable to read these formats correctly, so plain text remains the norm.

You can attach graphics to e-mail, of course, but it will depend on the recipient's set up whether those images are visible in the position you place them ('inline') or are merely attached to the end of the document. Placing large images inline is not recommended as it takes a long time to send (upload) and receive (download) large files. If you are sending a large file, whether text or graphics, you should compress it first using a 'zip' or compression program. Such programs are often pre-installed as part of your computer's operating system; if not you can download shareware or freeware versions from the Internet. Send the compressed file as an attachment to the e-mail message; it helps the recipient if you specify which compression program you used. The recipient has to decompress the file at the other end before viewing it.

Developments in e-mail software have tended to concentrate on introducing security and anti-nuisance features. It is possible to block junk e-mail messages and also to instruct the program to filter out anything that may contain certain words or subject matter. You can also use these facilities to organise your e-mail; getting the software to place incoming items into specific folders according to their sender or content, for example, rather than into a single inbox, which is the default (see *Filtering e-mail* for details).

E-mail addresses

E-mail addresses are the electronic equivalent of the 'pigeon holes' that used to be in every office mailroom. Each person has a unique address, which looks something like this:

fred@british-computers.co.uk
simon_watts@aol.com

The first part of the address usually shows the individual's or department's name; the second part (after the @) the company's name or the name of the Internet Service Provider (ISP). There is, however, no real restriction on what words or names you use, although you may be unable to use certain characters. Some ISPs, CompuServe in particular, use numbers instead of names: a typical CompuServe address looks like this 10846.253@compuserve.com.

If you are using e-mail at work, you will probably be given a specific address that is consistent with others in the organisation. If you run your own business, or use e-mail for personal business, you can select your own when you subscribe to the Internet via an ISP. There are millions of individuals and companies worldwide who already have addresses. and the Internet will not allow any name to be duplicated, so you may find that you have to try several alternatives before your choice is accepted, particularly if you are using your own name and have a common surname. For example, there may be more than one Bob Jones registered with your ISP. You can usually get around this by altering the format slightly; instead of calling yourself bob_jones@isp.co.uk, you could try one of the following:

bobjones@isp.co.uk
bob.jones@isp.co.uk
b_jones@isp.co.uk
jones_bob@isp.co.uk

Currently there are few e-mail directories around to let you look up a person's e-mail address; while there are some advertised on the Internet, they are not comprehensive and rely on that person having taken out an entry in the directory –

rather like the *Yellow Pages*. Therefore you must know a person's e-mail address before you can send them a message.

E-mail etiquette

Although e-mail is a recent development and is supposed to be fairly informal, the medium has built up a form of etiquette or code of conduct to ensure that receivers of e-mail do not take offence. (It is often referred to as 'Netiquette'.) The most important points of this are:

- Don't SHOUT. Using block capital letters is considered to be the equivalent of shouting. It's OK to use if you are sending an e-mail to the effect 'WE'VE GOT THE CONTRACT!' and you intend to convey excitement. Otherwise don't use block capitals.
- Don't 'flame'. Flaming is the equivalent of losing your temper or being overly aggressive, and usually results from someone reading a controversial comment and sending a hasty and ill-considered reply. Always read through your message before you send, and remove any angry or rude comments.
- Don't try to be funny or sarcastic. The same principle applies as with letters. E-mail does not translate humour very well because the person cannot see your face and it certainly does not translate sarcasm very well. And remember, once an e-mail has been sent, you cannot retrieve it. It is possible to use humour in personal e-mail to friends, especially if you indicate it with an appropriate emoticon (see later in this chapter).
- Always give the e-mail a title by filling in the 'Subject' line. It helps to tell the recipient what your e-mail is about before they open it, and it also helps you to file it correctly.
- Always check e-mail addresses are correct before sending. It is too easy to mistype an address, and many addresses are very similar, especially when sending to companies. Most e-mail software these days allows you to save e-mail addresses in an 'address book'; this is recommended for people with whom you regularly correspond as it saves a lot of typing and the potential for mistyping.

- Don't send anything confidential. Remember that e-mail can be easily read by other people. Anything private should be sent in a conventional sealed letter, not over the Internet.
- Don't use e-mail to hire or fire people; it is very bad manners. While there are now many Internet portal sites that advertise jobs and allow you to tender for work via the Internet, they should only ever be used for initial contact to exchange names, addresses and informal bids. Any advance should always be followed up with a conventional letter.
- When replying to someone, you can 'quote' parts of their original message. Insert this sign > before a line containing a quotation. Most e-mail software allows you to do this quite easily by selecting the Reply function; it then automatically copies the original email and places > in front of each line.

Writing and sending e-mail

Sending an e-mail is cheapest if you compose the message 'off-line'. That means typing out your e-mail before you connect to the Internet. That way you are not incurring charges while you mull over the content of your message. Obviously if your ISP offers free telephone usage or if you are using a company's Intranet this is less of an issue, but it is a good habit to get into.

When you select the function in your e-mail software that allows you to create a new message, a window will appear, similar to the one shown below.

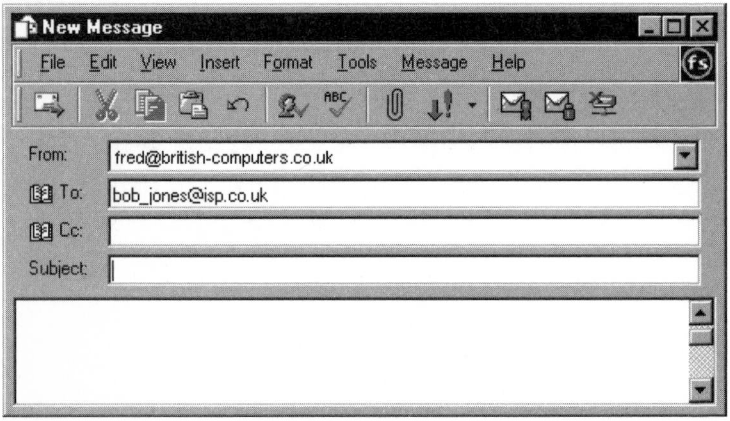

Figure 16: A typical e-mail message window

Your own e-mail address appears automatically in the From box (if you have more than one address, you may need to select the correct one from a drop-list). You will need to type or select the remaining information:

- Type the e-mail address of the recipient (in the preceding example bob_jones@isp.co.uk) in the To box, or select it from the address book if one exists.
- There is usually a separate area for the e-mail addresses of anyone else who needs a copy (in the example, this is the Cc box). Again, type or select from the address book.
- Type a subject or title for your note in the Subject box.
- Type your message in the main text box.
- To attach an image or other file, select the Attach function and specify the location of the file. You may need to repeat this step for each attachment: check your instruction manual for details. Remember to compress or 'zip' large files to minimise cost and the risk of the file becoming lost.

Once you have composed and checked your e-mail, you are ready to send it. You do not necessarily have to connect to the Internet immediately: in fact if you have several messages to send it is cheaper to write them all first, then send the whole batch at once. Your e-mail software should have the option of sending now or later; refer to the documentation if it is not clear how to do this. When you are ready to send your messages out, use the connection function to dial the ISP's server. Your software may then automatically send the files, or you may have to specifically ask it to do so: similarly it may receive files at the same time, or you may have to tell it to do so – unfortunately each e-mail application is different, so it is not possible to be specific here.

Once an e-mail has been despatched a copy is filed, usually in a 'Sent' file, for you to retrieve later if you wish. This copy contains the date and time of transmission for your records.

Receiving e-mail

Receiving messages is very simple. When you log on, your computer will usually tell you that you have received mail (you may have to ask it to check or to download it). This mail is usually placed in a 'Received' file or Inbox, although you can specify another location (see *Filtering e-mail*), from which you can read it, print it out, and delete it or move it elsewhere.

Dealing with unwanted e-mail

As with most communication systems these days, you may receive junk messages by e-mail, known in Internet jargon as 'spam'. This can be irritating and in some cases harmful; you may find you are being bombarded by pornography or even mail containing computer viruses. Junk e-mail usually results from leaving your e-mail address when you visit sites on the Internet, so if you avoid doing this, and enable the security functions of your e-mail and Internet software, the problem should be minimal.

Most e-mail systems now offer message filters that can be instructed to block messages containing certain material or words. You can blacklist companies or individuals once they have sent you an e-mail by putting their e-mail address into the block or filter option: any future e-mail sent from that address will be deleted before it reaches your screen.

Make sure you run virus-checking software on a regular basis. This will ensure that any e-mail you receive that contains a known virus will be identified quickly, allowing you to deal with it before it causes further harm. Make sure you download updates to the virus checker frequently, as new viruses are being developed all the time.

Filtering e-mail

As a result of the filtering options described above, you can now automate much of the filing of your e-mail; creating your own set of 'pigeon holes'. For example, you can specify that any e-mail received from fred@british-computers.co.uk is placed directly into a folder called Fred; or that any e-mail containing the word 'motorcycle', 'bike', 'race' or 'racing' is moved to the 'Bike racing' folder. The exact options available vary according to the software used.

E-mail jargon and symbols

As you would expect from a technological medium developed by software programmers, it hasn't taken long for e-mail and the Internet to develop a mysterious jargon all of their own. This includes abbreviations, acronyms and mnemonics; technical jargon describing program or service features; and emoticons, typed symbols that represent emotion – an attempt to overcome the misinterpretation that can occur without face-to-face or vocal interaction.

Common abbreviations

You may receive e-mail containing some of the following abbreviations :

FAQ	Frequently asked questions
BTW	By the way
AFAIK	As far as I know
IMHO	In my humble opinion
BBL	Be back later
RTFM	Read the flipping manual!
EML	Evil manic laugh

There are of course many more such abbreviations; new ones appear almost daily. Most of them are unsuitable for use in a business document and are more commonly used in personal e-mail. However, if you are working in a specific field of business such as chemicals, IT or printing, you may find there are abbreviations in frequent use that describe aspects of your work – these of course may not be restricted to use in e-mail. If you are unsure what one means, just ask the sender.

Technical jargon

The following jargon describes the technical features of e-mail or Internet usage:

Browser	The product you use to 'surf' the Internet, for example, Microsoft's Internet Explorer or Netscape's Communicator. They allow you to move around the Internet and view various pages.

Bookmarks	A browser function that allows you to store details of the pages on the Internet that you like and want to return to (some applications call these Favourites).
Attachment	A file that is sent with an e-mail message.
Cookie	A small text file used by websites to keep a record of visitors. When you visit a site a cookie is stored on your hard drive so the site recognises you when you return. The cookie also tells a site the names of the last few sites you visited and what type of browser you are using. It is supposed to be an advantage, for example, if you are registering for online shopping, as the cookie will provide your personal details and you don't have to type it out every time. However, it can result in unwanted e-mail ('spam'). If it worries you, you can instruct your browser not to accept cookies. Check your manual for the procedure.
Spam	Unwanted or junk e-mail. Like most junk mail, you are left wondering how the sender got hold of your name. The answer, as shown above, is through cookies; some spam results from other sources, in much the same way as junk mail, fax or telephone calls, but this is generally less common.
Portal	A website that offers services: for example, matching jobs to qualified experts or sellers to buyers.
BBS	A bulletin board service, where you can post messages and read messages from others on a specific topic. If you encounter technical jargon that you do not understand, it is a good idea to search for that term on the Internet. Alternatively use a good online technical dictionary, such as http://www.whatis.com or http://www.webopedia.internet.com.

Emoticons

Emoticons are little pictures created from punctuation. Sometimes they are called 'smileys' because when you see them on the screen at a certain angle they look like faces. Their purpose is to express emotion or intent, for example, happiness, sadness, anger or frustration, and thereby overcome the problem of the lack of face-to-face contact. While they are generally unsuitable for business communication, they are frequently used in more personal e-mail and on bulletin board postings, so it is worth listing the common ones here.

The most basic 'smileys' are so commonly used that some software automatically detects when you type this series of characters and changes it into a 'proper smiley', as shown below.

Happy   :) or :-) or ☺
Sad   :(or :-(or ☹
Only joking! (a wink)   ;) or ;-)
Bored   :0 or :-0
Angry or annoyed   :-| | or :-<
Crying   :'-(
Really happy   :-)) or :-D
Kiss   :-*
Surprised   :-o
Grim   :-|
Perplexed   :-/
Tongue-in-cheek   ;-^)

Of course there are many more – new ones come into being on an almost daily basis – but if you use a new one, your recipient might not understand it: the above are fairly well established. If you receive one that you don't understand, ask the sender!

CHAPTER 7

All about dictation

In this chapter we look at the subject of dictation. While maybe not as common these days as in previous decades, it is a method still much used in certain areas of business. We look at the reasons for this; the planning required for effective dictation; and methods of dictation, including new technologies.

Why dictate?

There are many reasons for using dictation. The most common would be:

- You may not have any keyboard skills.
- You may not have the time to write to a number of different people.
- You may not have access to a computer with suitable software, or even a typewriter.
- Your business environment may be structured so that you have to dictate letters to audio typists or face-to-face to secretaries or PAs.

In other words, you may not be able to avoid it.

Although dictating letters may seem very daunting at first, it should be a relatively simple procedure, providing you don't panic about articulating your thoughts. If you have never dictated before, use the planning method below to get started.

Planning for dictation

Dictating a letter requires different preparation to composing and writing a letter. For a start, you often have to think on your feet, composing the letter in your head and relaying it verbally almost simultaneously. Some people find this difficult and may need to make some planning notes before dictating.

There are several steps to take to make dictation as painless as possible for both yourself and your typist.

1. First, put together the correspondence of the businesses you are writing to and where possible the document you are replying to or something to provide the typist with the correct name and address.
2. Put these documents in the order in which you intend to tackle them, and number them. This way, all you have to say is 'Letter 1' and the typist will know that the document with this number contains the address and details required.
3. On a separate piece of paper, write down some brief notes by each number to remind you of what you want to say in each letter. This is for your benefit only; the typist will not see these notes. Here is an example of how your notes might look:

> 1) Findlay letter – not happy with quote – mention length of production time – suggest he rethinks – set time limit of one week for reply
> 2) Davidson e-mail – can make meeting on 4th – can we make it later? – reply ASAP
> 3) Hobson's fax – not happy with sales – need 10 per cent more next quarter – suggestions – schedule a meeting.

Figure 17: Typical dictation notes

The above examples might be fleshed out and dictated as follows. Here we have shown instructions to the typist with italics: you will have to signal these by the tone of your voice, and by leaving a pause before and after each instruction.

> *'Letter to John Findlay & Sons, Mr David Trimm – details on document 1.*
>
> Dear David, Thank you for your quote for the 3mm widgets, however, I am afraid that I am not happy with the time you are allowing for production. We need delivery at least two weeks earlier in order to meet our own deadlines.
>
> *(New paragraph)*
>
> Can I suggest that you rethink your quote and see whether

you can shorten your production time? I can give you a week to make the necessary adjustments then, regretfully, I will have to allow other companies to quote for the contract.

(New paragraph)

I hope that you understand our position. I look forward to hearing from you shortly.

Yours faithfully,

E-mail to Mark Davidson, Euromarketing plc. E-mail address is on document 2.

Mark,

I can make a meeting on the 4th but can we make the start-time a bit later? Say, 11 a.m. Please confirm this would be OK.

John.

Fax to Eric Hobson – his home fax number, copy to Managing Director.

Dear Eric,

I am a bit worried about the latest sales figures submitted last week. We need at least 10 percent more in this quarter in order to satisfy production requirements. I know that we have had a problem with illness among the salesforce but I feel that we should get together and have a meeting as soon as possible to discuss strategies. Ring my secretary and arrange a time next week. We can meet either here or at Head Office.

Regards,

John.

Figure 18: Typical dictation script

Just having a few notes as an *aide-memoire* can help you to dictate smoothly. It is particularly important if you are dictating several communications at different times while on the move – perhaps travelling around your sales area and not touching base for a few days. More and more business people who work from home actually dictate to themselves – in other words, they record instructions for their own benefit, for them to process on their computer when they get home. Even in this case it is important to be methodical. It is rather like writing yourself notes: it is infuriating if you scribble something in a hurry that makes sense at the time, but is meaningless a few days later.

Basic dictation

If you dictate your communications either face-to-face to an assistant or into a dictating machine, you must work out between the two of you the system that works best for you.

Be specific

The more that you as the originator of the communication can do to make your system efficient (as outlined at the beginning of this chapter), the quicker and more correct your returned transcripts will be. If you intend to rely on your assistant finding all the necessary documents and addresses then you need to be particularly specific in your instructions.

Use full names and locations

Example: Letter to John Davidson & Sons <u>of Rotherham</u>.
There could be another John Davidson & Sons in the file, or there could be several locations for John Davidson & Sons. You need to be specific about the location.

Give the job title

Example: For the attention of Mr Simon Watts, <u>Sales Director</u>.

Always give the job title, for two reasons. Firstly, some people are sensitive about not having their job title displayed on a letter and, secondly, there could be another Simon Watts in the company. If there is a father and son in the company with the same name, emphasise which one it is intended for.

Spell difficult words

Example: Letter to <u>Lesley Read</u> of <u>Knott-Howett Seams Ltd.</u>

Very important: spell out any difficult names, or names that could have more than one spelling. Be sensitive to the fact that some words or names can be misleading when heard rather than read. You cannot expect even the most efficient assistant to be able to spell a complicated foreign name, or to know whether the above surname should be Read, Reed, Reid or even Wread – let alone how to spell the company name!

Be considerate about the use of foreign or complex words. Do not litter your letters with pretentious words and phrases; plain English is always preferable. If you must insert technical terms or foreign words, spell them for your typist. This includes abbreviations: you need to indicate the case of each letter if it is important to the meaning. Look at this example of two very similar chemical abbreviations to see how important this is: Ca indicates calcium, while CA indicates citric acid, among other things.

Classify all documents

Example: Mark the letter Private & Confidential.

Always give clear instructions about confidentiality. Your regular typist may know that correspondence with this person is always confidential but your regular typist might be away, leaving someone else to deal with it.

Provide despatch instructions

Example: Send the letter by registered mail.

Always give instructions about despatch: do not assume that the person who will transcribe your dictation is familiar with routine procedures or aware that all correspondence with a particular company is time-sensitive.

Describe enclosures

Example: Enclose the blueprints which are in the file marked 'Bridge Development' – double-check with Mr Watkins in Sales that you have the correct plans before you enclose them.

Always give specific instructions to the typist about enclosures and if you are going to be absent for a while give a reference point, either someone dealing with your work in your absence or a date and time at which you can conduct a double check of important documents over the phone.

Instruct on dating and signing

Example: Date the letter the 25th March and sign it on my behalf please.

If you are dictating a batch of correspondence and sending it into your office at regular intervals, you need to give instructions about dating the letter and who is to sign in your absence.

Clearly separate instructions from text

Example: Start of letter.

Once you have given all the instructions for addressing, despatch and so on, you can then start the main text. Make sure the typist knows you have done this by explicitly stating it.

Be consistent

Set up a style of dictation and a system of transcribing, then stick to it. If you are slapdash in your dictating techniques then you only have yourself to blame if errors occur.

Speak clearly

There is no point in setting up a foolproof system of dictation and transcription if you are going to mumble all the way through it, so speak clearly.

Be courteous

Finally, always remember to say 'thank you' at the end of your batch of dictation. A little courtesy goes a long way towards generating co-operation and good teamwork.

Computer-assisted dictation

Recent developments in computer software has made it possible to work your computer by talking into it rather than typing commands. The range of some of this software is extraordinary. By attaching a special microphone, which you use as a hand-held dictation device, you can use your voice to control many applications including word-processing and other office tasks, voicemail, Internet telephony, video conferencing, and specialist tasks such as video editing, photo archiving, and giving presentations. Some microphones offer all the functions of a dictation device, offering buttons which play your voice back to you, record, fast forward and rewind.

Functions may include speech-to-text – you dictate your correspondence and it appears on the screen in the format you request – and text-to-speech – the computer reads back text you have typed or dictated, or which has been sent by someone else. Most applications offer a large vocabulary (100,000 to 300,000 words), and can be set to eliminate spelling or grammatical mistakes, correct incorrectly pronounced words, learn shortcuts, and so on. It is even possible to purchase a 'mobile' dictation package, which allows you to dictate using your laptop, listen to and edit your recorded speech, then e-mail it to your office for transcription. It is of course never safe to use such products while you are driving.

Several of these packages offer language translation. This subject is covered in the chapter *International correspondence*.

CHAPTER 8

The importance of preparation

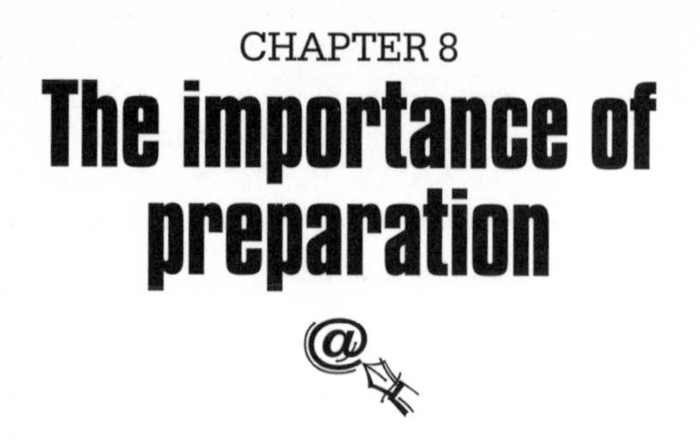

In this chapter we look at the preparation that should come before writing and sending a business letter or other communication; both mental and physical. Most of these items apply solely to letter-writing, as faxes and e-mail tend to be more informal. Preparation for dictation is discussed in the chapter *All about dictation*.

Mental preparation

Before putting pen to paper or fingers on a keyboard, you should always indulge in some mental preparation. It may sound like a waste of time but we are not talking about spending an hour preparing one single letter, just a few minutes carefully thinking of the objectives of the correspondence, the recipient and expressions it would be advisable or desirable to use. Consider how you want to project yourself, and whether you are expressing yourself clearly.

The aim of the correspondence

Despite the variety of topics on which business correspondence is written, each communication has at least one of three purposes: to convey information; to prompt action; or to maintain a satisfactory working relationship. The purpose is likely to affect the tone and style of your communication, so it is important to keep the general aim in mind, as well as any more specific intent. A sales letter will obviously be more upbeat in tone than a press release that merely conveys information, facts and figures. A letter of complaint can vary in tone depending upon whether it is an initial approach or the third one you have sent to a company that is not performing to your satisfaction. A letter opening negotiations between you and a prospective client should convey respect and reliability and inspire confidence from the reader. So you see how important it is to spend some time thinking about the tone of your letter and the language you will use, before you start to write.

The recipient

Anything you know about your correspondent or their business can help you write a more effective letter. Try to put yourself in your correspondent's shoes. This may suggest ways in which you can frame your letter and what words you might use. Never assume that because the person you are writing to is a jokey, informal type that this is the way to discuss your business by letter. Quite often, the business persona can be a complete contrast to someone's relaxed 'at-home' persona. Humour and informality are generally not a part of business communication, even if you know the recipient personally,so keep it businesslike.

Clarity of thought and expression

The importance of organising your thoughts and noting down the main points before writing or replying to a letter is stressed throughout this book. It is also important that, having decided what you want to say, you express yourself in a way the recipient will understand. Try to use short words and short sentences which convey the message simply and clearly. Long words and complex constructions are more difficult to read and are often imprecise. If you do sometimes use long words – they cannot always be avoided – get into the habit of checking their meaning and spelling in a dictionary. It is suprising how often they do not convey quite the meaning you intended. Only use technical jargon when you are speaking to another technician in your field.

Similarly, try not to use quasi-legal phrases, such as 'subject to' or 'we reserve the right', which sound threatening and are generally meaningless. (These days even lawyers are being encouraged to write in plain English wherever possible.) Avoid foreign phrases where a straightforward English equivalent is available: you want the recipient to understand your letter, not marvel at your knowledge.

Some long or complex words and phrases and shorter simpler alternatives with which you can replace them are given in the appendix *Troublesome words and phrases* at the back of this book. A brief summary of English usage – grammar, punctuation, spelling and so on – can be found in the chapter *Writing well*.

What to avoid

Try not to use phrases such as 'We beg to acknowledge receipt of your letter' or 'assuring you of our best attention'. These are clichés and usually add little to your meaning. Many of these phrases are a relic from the age of the quill pen when manners were very formal and always expressed in letters. Today it is better to think how you would express an idea if you were talking face-to-face with the person. This is often a good way of avoiding commercialese, since few people would say to a new client 'I am assuring you of our best attention' – they would more likely say 'You can be certain that we put our customer's needs first all the time' or even ' We try to always do our best for our customers'. A list of typical clichés and their simpler alternatives is given in the appendix *Troublesome words and phrases* at the back of this book.

Courtesy and honesty

These qualities are important in a letter not merely because they are the correct way to behave but also because you are committing yourself to paper. If you wrote anything libellous, for example, you may well end up in court. Remember that the person to whom you are writing may not be the only one who reads the letter. Beware particularly with faxes and e-mail as they cannot be sealed and marked for a particular person's attention only. If you are writing a letter of complaint, think very carefully before choosing your words. Try not to be abusive, but if you simply must get it off your chest, then write it out and leave it unsent for a day. When you calm down, you may find the letter seems too harsh after all.

Never try to fudge an issue in a letter. Never tell lies about anything, particularly the state of your company's finances or ability to do certain jobs. Many a businessman has been convicted of fraud or misrepresentation due to the content of a letter.

Present yourself in the best light

A business communication says a great deal about you and your company and it is all done with your choice of words and the tone you adopt. If you project dignity, good intentions, consideration and honesty in your letters you will be doing more public relations work for your company than any consultancy could. The letters you send to your colleagues and employees should be considerate, accurate and easily understandable; the letters you send to your customers should be reassuring, honest and easily understandable; while the letters you send to those who have defaulted against your company should be dignified and regretful. Even letters that terminate employment, apologise for your company's transgressions or threaten legal action can be phrased in such a way that they help a situation, not fan the flames of mistrust and misunderstanding.

Physical preparation

Next, consider physical preparation; whether to make some notes for yourself to then expand, or a longhand draft for a secretary to type up, or an *aide-memoire* for later dictation. (Dictation is also covered in detail in the chapter *All about dictation.*)

You need a basic plan – a bit like a shopping list – to make sure that you don't forget essential components of the communication. Looking at the points highlighted above, write down:

- to whom the letter is to be addressed, and the subject of the letter
- the aim of the communication
- any points you want to raise, in their order of priority
- what you think the tone of the letter should be
- any special instructions about the despatch of the communication.

This should take you no more than five minutes, and should result in something like this:

Letter to:	*Vegas Hotel re. Seminar booking*
Purpose:	*To confirm booking and make sure they have the details right*
Salient points:	*Make sure they know that everyone needs single rooms – no sharing* *Everyone is having breakfast and dinner – no lunch* *Seminar room should be reserved for forty people for three days (give dates)* *Make sure seminar room has telephone, fax, overhead projector, TV, video and coffee machine installed.* *Ask for confirmation in writing.*
Tone :	*Brisk, friendly and appreciative*
Despatch:	*E-mail and fax to Mr E Woodlands, Business Manager.*

Figure 19: Typical preparatory notes

This provides a template that can be fleshed out into a letter by you or an informed and experienced PA (who won't need any further instruction than the notes above). The notes provide a starting point, whether you intend writing a draft for your secretary or typist or tackling it yourself. The same notes can be used as an *aide-memoire* if you are dictating a letter on a machine to be typed up later by someone else.

Obtain all relevant addresses, fax numbers and e-mail addresses before you make a start on the letter. If you are dictating or drafting for someone else to type up then either have addresses ready for that person – and, if there are several letters to be done, have the information in the correct order – or know that they can be found in the filing system.

CHAPTER 9

Making a start

Often, the most difficult thing to do is actually start a letter and in this chapter we simply give you some alternatives for doing just that – phrases that are standard business letter openings.

Salutations

The salutation you use will depend on the form of address you have selected, depending upon the person's position or rank, your relationship with that person, the formality of the letter and so on. Correct forms of address are discussed in general terms in the chapter *Structure, layout and style*; details of how to address specific military, religious, noble or royal personages are given in the appendix *Ceremonious forms of address*, at the back of this book.

In general, the following rules apply:

If addressed to ...	*Start with ...*	*Style*
An unnamed recipient, a person of office (such as an MP), or a person of unknown sex	Dear Sir Dear Madam Dear Sir or Madam	formal
An entire company or department	Dear Sirs Dear Mesdames*	formal
An individual	Dear Mr/Mrs/Ms Jones**	formal
	Dear Anne Jones	less formal
A colleague or peer	Dear Arthur	even less formal

Someone you know personally	Dear Mary	informal
A friend	Dearest Emily	personal

* Only to be used if the entire company or department consists of female staff: if there is a mixture, the correct form is 'Dear Sirs'.

** Note the use of courtesy title and surname, but no initials or first names. The use of a first name indicates a greater degree of informality, or may be used where the person's sex is unknown. In general, it is best to consider how you would address the recipient in person, and use that form.

Opening lines

The opening line you use will depend on the reason for the letter, the formality of the letter, and whether it is a reply to a previous letter.

First-time openings

The openings suggested here are mainly for use in first-contact letters or, perhaps, for following up a first meeting. They assume that you know little if anything about the reader, and that you have had no prior formal communication.

I am the Sales Manager of ...
I would like to introduce myself and my company ...
We would like to offer your company an opportunity to ...
We are a small company that manufactures ...
We think that we have a product that you may be interested in ...
We met recently at ... and you indicated that you might be interested in ...
You gave me your details [or card] recently at ... and I am writing to give you details of ...
We are currently doing some work for a company in your field and we wondered whether ...
We understand that you are currently looking for ...
I wonder if you might be interested in ...
We have a great deal of experience in ...
I am sure that you have heard of our company ...
I am writing to enquire about ...

I would like to offer your company ...
I would like to invite you to a ...
May I take this opportunity to ...

Follow-up letters

This is a letter of reply, which is your written confirmation of a communication you have received, a conversation or a telephone discussion. Typical opening lines include:

Further to your fax/letter/invoice/e-mail dated ...
Further to our discussion of last Wednesday ...
Further to our telephone conversation, I am writing to confirm that ...
Further to your recent conversation/discussion/telephone conversation with ...
Further to your request for...

You could also use the word 'following' as in :

Following our recent conversation, I would like to emphasise/confirm/reject ...
Following our meeting last week, I am writing to confirm ...
Following our last telephone conversation/discussion/e-mail exchange ...

Alternatively, you could 'refer' to the previous activity:

With reference to your telephone call of yesterday ...
With reference to the discussion that took place at Head Office last week ...
With reference to the above [meaning the title of the communication] ...

If sending a fax or e-mail, both of which can be more brief and informal, you could use the form 'Re:':

Re: Your outstanding payment for ...
Re: the recent vacancy discussed ...
Re: the latest sales figures received ...

You may use the word 'confirm' if the purpose of your 'follow-up' letter is to do just that:

I am writing to confirm that we are agreed on the terms outlined in our meeting ...

I confirm that your faxed quotation is acceptable to this company …
I would like to confirm our order …
This letter is to confirm our meeting on 12th August, at 14:00 at your offices …
I wish to confirm the points we discussed over the telephone …
I wish to confirm that our company is interested in proceeding with your suggestions……….

Or you can just dispense with preamble altogether, and go straight to the point:

It was agreed at the meeting held on 12th August at 14:00 …
As discussed earlier this week……….
As we agreed today, I would like to emphasise …

You may prefer to start your follow-up letter with a polite 'thank you':

Thank you for sending us the …
Thank you for your letter of the 12th February …
Thank you for the cheque you sent on 20th March …
Thank you for coming to see me last Wednesday …
Thank you for quoting for the above order [where the title shows the order number] …
Thank you for your recent enquiry …
Thank you for your application for the position of …

Letters of praise or goodwill

It is a sad fact that many managers neglect to find time to send letters of praise but can always find time to send letters of censure. The letter of praise is always an effective and economical method of achieving good staff morale and good customer relations. There are other letters – that may not include praise – in which you would want to transmit a pleasurable, positive feeling. Examples of opening lines include:

I would like to say how delighted I am that …
Congratulations to all your department on …
I would like to offer my personal thanks for …
I am pleased to announce that …
I am delighted to be able to tell you …
Thank you to all of you who have …

I am pleased to confirm that ...
It was a pleasure to ...
It was great talking to you last week ...
I am writing to extend my best wishes ...
I am writing to say how much I enjoyed ...
I am writing to thank you for your splendid efforts on behalf of our company ...
I wish to extend my appreciation..........
May I say how much I appreciated..........
Please accept my heartfelt thanks..........
Please convey to your staff my appreciation of..........

And so on. There are so many variations; what a shame they are not more commonly used.

Letters of disapproval or dissatisfaction

There are occasions when you wish to convey to the recipient of your letter your disapproval, annoyance, disappointment or some other negative emotion. Here the opening line is very important, as it sets the tone of what is to follow and leaves the reader in no doubt, from the start, that you are unhappy. You might use one of the following:

I am dismayed at the lack of response to my previous letter ...
I am disappointed at the quality of ...
I am very disappointed with your lack of effort ...
I regret to inform you that I am not happy with ...
I am at a loss to understand why you have ....
I had hoped that this letter would not be necessary, however ...
I am afraid that, due to recent events, I have to officially write and tell you that ...
I am writing to express my dissatisfaction of ...
I am writing, with regret, to inform you that ...
I am writing, with some concern, to enquire why ...
I am writing on a matter which is causing me some concern ...
It is with regret that I must inform you ...
I was disturbed/concerned/unhappy/shocked to learn ...

Letters of apology or regret

It is important to convey and emphasise the appropriate emotion in the first line, so that the reader will continue to read the communication. Letters of apology may start like this:

My apologies for the delay in …
My sincere apologies in not responding to your request with more speed …
I am sorry that you have not received the …
I cannot apologise enough for the problems you outlined in your letter …
I am very sorry to hear that you are dissatisfied with …
Please accept my apologies for …
We were disturbed to learn that …
We wish to apologise for our lack of attention in this matter …
We would like to offer our apology for this delay in despatch …
Owing to …, we must apologise to those customers who …
May we offer from the outset our sincere apologies for any inconvenience caused …

Letters of regret also need to present the facts immediately, but need to be softened by a good closure, which we will examine in the next chapter. Suggested openings are:

I regret to inform you that …
I regret to announce that …
I am sorry to have to tell you this but …
I am sorry to be the one to inform you that …
I regret to say that …
I am sorry but our company feels that …

Letters of condolence

These letters need to be very carefully phrased so as not to cause any distress. Suggested openings are as follows:

We were deeply shocked by the death of …
May we offer our condolences …
I am saddened by the death of …
Please accept my sincere condolences …
Please accept my sympathies for your loss …
We were very sorry to hear your sad news …
Our thoughts are with you at this sad time …
The company has felt the loss of … deeply …

An example of this type of letter is shown in the chapter *Writing to employees and employers*, in the section *Examples of letters from employer to employee*.

What to aim for

There are obviously many ways to start a letter successfully. The main point is to consider what reaction you wish to induce in the recipient, and to place the trigger for that reaction in your opening line, following an appropriate salutation. Then you can go into further detail in the body of the letter.

CHAPTER 10

Signing off

Next to starting a letter, the most difficult thing is to finish it effectively. Once again, the way in which you do so depends upon the relationship you have demonstrated in the letter itself. There are two elements to finishing a letter: an ending, called the closing line; and an appropriate sign-off, called the complimentary close. In this chapter, we look at these in detail, and also look at the final checks to be made to a letter before posting.

Ending on the right note

It is important in business letters to make your point clearly, particularly at the start and at the end, so that your reader is aware of what it is you want. For example, with a follow-up letter you generally want to encourage the relationship to continue and so you would give it a very different finish from a letter of complaint, where the ending of the letter would demand action, a remedy or an apology. In this section we look at various options for the final line of a letter, to ensure you get your point across.

Endings that encourage further communication

There are several encouraging endings you can use. A number of useful examples are shown below.

I look forward to hearing from you in the near future ...
I look forward to our further discussion ...
I look forward to another meeting ...
I look forward to receiving your quote ...
I look forward to seeing you soon ...
If you have any problems/questions please contact me ...

If you need further information, please let me know ...
If you would like another meeting ...
If you are interested in these proposals ...
If you are still unable to resolve the matter please contact me ...
Let me know if I can be of further assistance ...
Let me know if you think another meeting would be productive ...
Let me know if you have any reservations about the above ...
Let me know if you need any further information ...
I hope to hear from you soon ...
I hope that this is satisfactory ...
I hope that you have all the information necessary ...
I hope that you feel it has been worthwhile ...
I trust that the above meets with your approval ...
I trust that you can now put together a new plan ...
I trust that you have all the specifications you need ...
I trust this is satisfactory ...
Please call me if you need any further advice ...
Please contact me if you need further assistance ...
Please fax your requirements as soon as possible ...
Please confirm by return ...
Would you please confirm receipt of ...
Would you please contact my office to make another appointment ...
Would you please acknowledge delivery dates ...
Thanking you in anticipation of ...

Endings that demand action

When you have sent a letter of complaint or disapproval and you wish to emphasise the seriousness of your purpose, you need to end with a firm admonition. There are several acceptable ways to do this, some of which are shown below.

I trust that this matter will be dealt with as soon as possible ...
I trust that this will not arise again ...
I trust that this is the last we shall hear of the matter ...
I trust that you will rectify these mistakes at once ...
Please confirm that you have solved all the outstanding problems ...
Please contact me as soon as possible ...
Please do not let this matter arise again ...

Please amend your files accordingly ...
Please confirm receipt of this letter ...
Please do not write to me again ...
I hope this is an end of the matter ...
I hope you will take my suggestions on board without delay ...
I hope you will rectify the matter at once ...
I hope there will be no further occurrence of this error ...
I hope you will resolve the matter immediately ...
I expect a full apology ...
I expect action to be taken immediately ...
I expect a full report as soon as possible ...
I expect no further occurrence of this problem ...

Endings that suggest further action

Use this type of ending when you hope for a response, but are not demanding or asking for one. It is appropriate for sales letters and first-contact letters. Some examples are given below.

If you are interested in further information, please call ...
If I can be of any further assistance, please ...
If you would like a demonstration, please ...
If you would like to know more, please ...
If you would like to place an order, please ...
I hope that we can be of further assistance ...
I hope that you will decide to take the matter further ...
I hope you will consider another meeting ...
I hope that we have helped you in this matter ...
Please give the matter some thought ...
Please consider my proposal ...
Please bear us in mind should you require ...
Please keep our details on file for future reference ...
Please keep us in mind should you wish to ...
Do not hesitate to contact us should you ...
Do not hesitate to ask us for further information ...
Do not hesitate to give us a call if you ...
Do not hesitate to take up references ...

Endings that are simply polite

A polite ending is a general way of ending a letter on a gracious note. It is merely a thank you and in general does not imply that there should be a response. For example:

Thank you for your co-operation ...
Thank you for your interest ...
Thank you for your help ...
Thank you for your assistance ...
Thank you for your attention ...

The following polite endings do suggest that you are expecting a response:

Thanking you in advance ...
Thanking you in anticipation of your assistance [or help, response].

Signing off your letter

It is important to use the correct complimentary close, or sign-off, in a business letter. It is possible to offend your reader by being too friendly or too formal, even though the rest of the letter may be perfect in tone and style.

The way you sign off a letter can generally be dictated by the way you started it:

If you started ...	*Sign off with ...*	*Style*
Dear Sir or Madam	Yours faithfully	formal
Dear Mr/Mrs/Ms Jones	Yours sincerely	less formal
Dear Arthur	Yours truly	even less formal
Dear Mary	Regards	informal, to someone you know personally
Dear Andy	With kind regards*	informal, to someone you know and like
Dearest Emily	With best wishes**	personal, to a friend

* This could also be 'Kind regards', 'Kindest regards', 'Warmest regards' or 'Best regards'.
** This could also be simply 'Best wishes'.

If writing to a person of title, with military, religious, ceremonial or royal status, it is even more important to use the correct form of address and sign-off to avoid giving offence. For full details of these, see the appendix *Ceremonious forms of address* at the back of this book.

The final check

Once a letter has been written, it must be checked. If you have written it yourself, remember to proofread it, not just for spellings but also for references, facts, figures, times, dates, addresses and names. If someone else has written it for you, ask them to return the finished letter and any attachments to you, with the information you gave them regarding the recipient's address. Check everything as listed above, and ensure that they have understood your instructions properly (particularly if working from your handwritten draft); attached all the required attachments; got the name, title and address correct; and understood any instructions you have given about despatch.

CHAPTER 11

Business-to-business correspondence

In this chapter, we look at letters commonly written from one business to another. Getting these right is important, as it shows the professionalism of your organisation. Subjects covered include: writing letters to obtain goods or credit from a supplier; asking for and providing trade references; and ordering and returning goods.

There are of course many other letters that one business may need to write to another. Some of these are included in other chapters of this book, for example, the chasing of debts is discussed in the chapter *Awkward letters*, as is the writing of letters of complaint or refusal; while the writing of promotional material, such as sales letters, is discussed in the chapter *Writing effective promotional material*.

Writing to suppliers

This falls into two broad categories: writing to a new, prospective supplier, and writing to an existing supplier.

Writing to potential suppliers

If you are in the business of retail or distribution, you may on occasion need to write to a company to request their catalogue or offer to stock their goods, or to place an order. While this is often done by telephone, a written approach is always welcomed, and provides you with a record of all dealings. Here we offer some examples of how such letters should be framed.

Asking for details of a product range

Greenfingers Garden Supplies Ltd
Mill Lane
DROSFORD
Wilts
DO4 7NB

5 June 2000

Umow Lawnmowers Ltd
54-58 Fern Road
TIPLON
West Midlands
B16 7AJ

Dear Sirs

Please send us a catalogue of your full lawnmower range, and supply us with details regarding trade terms.

At the same time perhaps you could tell us how soon we might expect delivery after placing an order, and what the position is regarding after-sales service.

Yours faithfully
Greenfingers Garden Supplies Ltd

Richard Miles

Placing a first order

Goodbooks
18 Middens Way
EAST RENICK
Strathclyde
RE5 8JT

4 May 2000

Henry & Jones (Publishers) Ltd
42 Parade Street
EDINBURGH
ED1 6DH

Dear Sirs

Please supply the following books as listed in your January to July 2000 catalogue.

Quantity	Title	Author	ISBN
3	Metaphysical Plurality	Junkett	28975 9
5	Scientific Communication	Duncan and Yole	34661 9
10	Music in the 19th Century	Nicol	28975 8

I understand that you will supply these books on a sale or return basis at a discount of 25% but that I will be liable for carriage.

Yours faithfully

Helen Baird (Mrs)

Providing references to a potential supplier

Maxi Components Limited
LECHFORD
Bucks
SL8 91V

Your ref JPQ/7/82
Our ref PJ/S/70

8 July 2000

Mr Peter Wood
Marston Metal Supplies
Long Lane
MARSTON
Northants
LB7 91N

Dear Mr Wood

Thank you for your letter of 4 July. Please contact either our branch of Midwest Bank plc, or Sankey Smith & Co Ltd, for the reference you require. Their addresses are as follows:

Mr John Wilson (Manager)
Midwest Bank plc
The Parade
LECHFORD
Bucks
SL8 8RT

Sankey Smith & Co Ltd
Unit 4
Beechfield Trading Estate
WALTON
Lancs
NR4 6BW

Yours sincerely

Peter Jones

Writing to existing suppliers

If you deal with a supplier on a regular basis, you probably use preprinted order forms or order by telephone. However, there are some situations in which you need to write a letter, such as when returning goods, complaining about the quality of goods or the level of service you have received, or when an error has been made in an invoice issued to you. Here are some examples of how such letters could be framed.

Returning unwanted goods

Goodbooks
18 Middens Way
EAST RENICK
Strathclyde
RE5 8JT

4 May 2000

Henry & Jones (Publishers) Ltd
42 Parade Street
EDINBURGH
ED1 6DH

Dear Sirs

We have today received from you a package containing books that we have not ordered:

Quantity	Title	Author	ISBN
9	GCSE French sample tests	Smith	28985 8
1	Down the River	Armsby, Joan	34064 9

Goodbooks specialises in music publications, so would be unable to sell these books. Would you therefore arrange for these to be collected, or send details of how to return them to you without incurring the cost of carriage.

Yours faithfully

Helen Baird (Mrs)

Advising of invoicing errors

It is not unknown for even computerised accounting systems to produce the strangest of errors. If you receive a bill from a supplier containing details of unknown goods, goods that you did not receive or goods you returned, or merely an inaccurate calculation, you should respond as quickly as possible to ensure the error is corrected. Do not be overly critical in your letter; everyone makes mistakes, although if you are on the receiving end of many an incorrect invoice from the same supplier, it is probably worth making a separate complaint.

MicroFold Ltd
READING
Berks
HY5 1SC

1 December 2000

Accounts Department
Myers Wholesale Ltd
LUDLEY
Wilts
YT7 4ST

Dear Sirs

We have this morning received your invoice XY76467, dated 25 November.

The second item on this invoice is for two hundred rubber hose clips, at a total cost of £24.86. These items were on our original order IR62534, but were later cancelled in writing on 25 November. We assume that you did receive this cancellation as the items were not delivered with the rest of the goods and did not appear on the delivery note.

We are therefore returning your invoice for amendment. When we receive the corrected version, we shall send payment by return.
Yours faithfully

Michael Cardon
Accounts Payable
Enc.

(Don't forget to enclose the invoice, plus copies of your original order and any other correspondence.)

Complaining about goods or services received

It is important not to be seen as a tiresome moaner, but to make your points constructively, to engender sympathy and regret in the recipient, to get the desired result.

In the chapter *Awkward letters* you will find some general advice on writing letters of complaint, together with some examples.

Writing to retailers and customers

If you are a supplier, or a retailer with trade customers, you will often need to write to them. For example, if a retailer or customer orders or returns goods that you are unable to supply, or if they return goods in a condition that you are unable to accept. Other situations that are not specific to inter-business communications, such as the chasing of debts and answering of letters of complaint, are covered in the chapter *Awkward letters*; while promotional letters, such as those you send out to advise of a sale or special offer, are covered in the chapter *Writing effective promotional material*.

Sending details of products

Umow Lawnmowers Ltd
54-58 Fern Road
TIPLON
West Midlands
B16 7AJ

10 June 2000

Mr Richard Miles
Greenfingers Garden Supplies Ltd
Mill Lane
DROSFORD
Wilts
DO4 7NB

Dear Mr Miles

Thank you for your letter of 5 June.

We have pleasure in enclosing our catalogue of lawnmowers. Spares for all current models are readily available from us, and we also operate a regular free collection and delivery repair service for our dealers.

Our terms are 30 days nett from date of invoice.

We normally hope to make deliveries within three to four weeks of receipt of order. However, I am afraid that delivery of Model TE7 may take up to six weeks, due to production difficulties. We hope, however, to resolve these problems within the next couple of months.

Our Southern Representative, Mr John Spears of 15 Rose Way, Gromsey, Hants (telephone Gromsey 45219) would, of course, be pleased to call on you at your request.

Yours sincerely

Harry Treen
Sales Department

Requesting trade/bank references

Marston Metal Supplies
Long Lane
MARSTON
Northants
LB7 91N

Your ref PJ/M/69
Our ref JPQ/7/82

4 July 2000

Peter Jones Esq
Managing Director
Maxi Components Limited
LECHFORD
Bucks
SL8 91V

Dear Mr Jones

Thank you for your order of 28 June, which is receiving our prompt attention.

Since this is the first occasion on which you have placed an order with us, we would be grateful if you could furnish us with your banker's or a trade reference. Alternatively we would be happy to receive your remittance before despatch of your order.

Yours sincerely
Marston Metal Supplies

Peter Wood

Advising of inability to supply

Marston Metal Supplies
Long Lane
MARSTON
Northants
LB7 91N

Your ref PJ/M/69
Our ref JPQ/7/82

4 July 2000

Peter Jones Esq
Managing Director
Maxi Components Limited
LECHFORD
Bucks
SL8 91V

Dear Mr Jones

Thank you for your order of 28 June. Unfortunately we are no longer able to supply the black anodised aluminium you require, because of new government safety regulations concerning the use of chemicals involved in the anodising process. May I refer you, however, to the following company, which imports a similar product that does not infringe these regulations:

National Metallic Ltd
Spitfields Way
Broiton
Yorks
NW2 8DX

I apologise for this inconvenience, and hope that we may continue to supply your other aluminium requirements.

Yours sincerely
Marston Metal Supplies

Peter Wood

Advising of inability to accept returned goods

Umow Lawnmowers Ltd
54-58 Fern Road
TIPLON
West Midlands
B16 7AJ

Our ref: HS/IEN/99
10 June 2000

Mr Richard Miles
Greenfingers Garden Supplies Ltd
Mill Lane
DROSFORD
Wilts
DO4 7NB

Dear Mr Miles

I have today received your package containing four lawnmower blades that you state to be faulty.

I understand from your letter that these were found unsuitable on delivery and are being returned for refund. However, close inspection of the blades indicates that they have been used on at least one occasion, and the damage appears to have resulted from running the machine into concrete, or a similar compound, as traces of this can be seen on the cutting edge.

For this reason, we are unable to offer a refund, as the damage was not present when the goods left these premises.

If you have any further comments on this matter, or wish us to return the blades to you, please write to this department, quoting the reference above, within the next 30 days. If we do not hear from you by this date, the goods will be disposed of.

Yours sincerely

Harry Treen
Sales Department

Refusing to offer credit

Marston Metal Supplies
Long Lane
MARSTON
Northants
LB7 91N

Our ref JPQ/3/84
4 July 2000

Mr A Dettor
Shepherd's Cottage
Walken Way
OCFORD
Berks
RG2 8FG

Dear Mr Dettor

Thank you for your order of 28 June.

We are unfortunately unable to offer you credit terms at this time.

Should you wish to continue with this order, please forward a cheque or bank draft for the balance, or telephone us to arrange payment by credit or debit card.

Yours sincerely
Marston Metal Supplies

Peter Wood

Writing to banks

You may, on occasion, need to write to the company's bankers, for example to arrange a loan, or to ask them to provide a banker's reference for a supplier. Here are examples of each.

Requesting credit facilities

Umow Lawnmowers Ltd
54-58 Fern Road
TIPLON
West Midlands
B16 7AJ

10 June 2000

E R Cox Ltd
Small Business Manager
Big Bank plc
High Street
TIPLON
West Midlands
B15 8AG

Dear Mr Cox

ACCOUNT NO 19274364

We would like to arrange for a temporary working overdraft of £4,000 on the above account.

We are currently importing from Asia parts made to our specific order, for which payment is required in advance. Until the goods arrive and are despatched to the customer we are unable to bill for them, and even after this date must offer our usual terms of 30 days. While our account balance is currently healthy, we will be closing for two weeks during September, so the drop in revenue during this time added to the above problem may cause us to become overdrawn.

Either of our directors would be pleased to come and discuss this matter with you, if you wish.

Yours sincerely

Joan Juston
Accounts Manager

Requesting a banker's reference

This example shows how to ask a bank to provide a reference for a potential customer.

Marston Metal Supplies
Long Lane
MARSTON
Northants
LB7 91N

13 July 2000

MidWest Bank plc
Fenton Street
WINTON
Northants
NR4 6BW

Dear Sirs

We have received an order from Maxi Components Limited of Lechford, who wish to open a credit account with us.

This is the first instance of our trading with this company, who have supplied your name as their bankers. Please let us know, in confidence, whether this company would be reliable for a credit arrangement of up to £1,000 per month, payable within 30 days.

Yours faithfully
Marston Metal Supplies

Peter Wood

CHAPTER 12

Writing to employees and employers

The area of business correspondence that requires the most delicacy is that between employees, or potential employees, and their employers. Modern employment law considers all written communication between employer and employee to have legal status, and therefore legal implications. Care must therefore be taken to comply with the law, not give offence, and promote good relationships.

In this chapter we discuss such communication, and offer suggestions for how to improve it. Some example letters are provided.

Writing to employees

There are several areas of concern when drafting employee communications. We will deal with the simplest first – that of promoting good relations with the workforce.

Promoting good employee relations

'Management by memo' is usually a term of criticism because it means that managers neglect to communicate with their employees face-to-face, preferring to do so in writing. This can provoke hostility in the workforce but obviously there are certain occasions when face-to-face discussions are not practical, where one must resort to written communications. Similarly, there are some situations that must be dealt with face-to-face, at least initially.

When not to write

A letter should never be the first communication in the following circumstances :

- When giving a first warning of unsatisfactory work. A verbal warning is the first step in the legal procedure for dismissal.
- When giving second and subsequent warnings. While written warning is required by law, it should be prefaced with a verbal indication that it is being issued.
- When dismissing an employee, whatever the reason. The law requires an official written notice of dismissal, but you should always tell the person face-to-face that this is what you are going to do.
- When giving notice of redundancy.
- When giving notice of early retirement, including early retirement due to long-term illness.
- When giving notice of a change of job or responsibilities, or salary level.
- When informing an employee of complaints about him or her from other employees.
- When criticising an employee, even constructively. Do this face-to-face, but never in the presence of the employee's peers.
- When praising an individual employee for good work. Try to praise in the presence of others whenever possible.

There are numerous other situations that could occur – private, confidential or potentially traumatic – that should never be dealt with in written form as the first approach, if at all.

Nevertheless, there are occasions where, for example, you have a company announcement to make and there are just too many employees spread over too many locations for a face-to-face announcement to be practical. In this instance you need to resort to the memo.

Writing good staff memos

Sending a bad memo, one that is terse, doesn't give all the facts, does not show management in a sympathetic light and irritates or infuriates the staff, is worse than not sending a memo at all. Here are some guidelines for more effective communication:

1. Background.
   Never assume that the employees know the background to the memo, but do not assume that they are totally ignorant either. Start your memo with a paragraph like this:
   'Some of you may be aware that for some time the company has been negotiating with A.N. Other Ltd to merge our resources and try to capture a bigger share of the fresh food market. These discussions have been taking place over the last few weeks and we are now in a position to tell employees the outcome.'

2. Reassurance.
   If you are in a position to do so, inject a note of reassurance into the memo as soon as possible. For example:
   'We realise that some of you will be concerned about the possible loss of jobs but we would like to reassure you that there will be no job losses in the foreseeable future.'
   Even if your memo is very bad news, you can usually find some reassuring words. For example, if your company is closing down, tell them at this point how you will be helping them financially or towards other employment.

3. Outline changes.
   Next, outline any possible changes that may take place. For example:
   'On the contrary, we feel that this merger will open up new opportunities for some existing staff to increase their responsibilities and we will be talking to you about specific plans in due course.'

4. Give facts.
   Then give any relevant facts:
   'Once the two companies have merged (which will take roughly two months) we will operate from seven depots, instead of our current four, with a total workforce of 800 and a fleet of 97 vehicles.'

5. What to do now.

   Next, give information about how to proceed on receiving the memo.

   'Therefore, until you receive further notification from the management, please carry on your work as before. If you have any queries or concerns, please talk to your supervisors and they will endeavour to help you.'

6. Final words.

   End the memo by expressing thanks, consideration, regret or apology – as appropriate to the situation.

   Whether the memo is upbeat or imparts less welcome news, the principles remain the same. If you follow these guidelines you should present yourself in a good light and foster good employer/employee relations – even if the news you are giving in your written communication is very bad.

To recap:

1. Background
2. Reassurance
3. Outline changes
4. Give facts
5. What to do now
6. Final words – thanks, regret or apology.

Avoid causing offence

This sounds obvious, but in fact it is all too easy to offend nowadays, and this can have legal implications. Modern culture has taught many people to be constantly on the defensive and alert for any criticism, intended or not. When writing letters to employees, heed the following advice:

Humour

Never attempt to use humour in communication with employees: it may not be appreciated. In certain cases it could be considered inflammatory. Not everyone has the same sense of humour; some people do not have a sense of humour at all. It is easy to give offence by trying to be funny. You may be a naturally funny person, the life and soul of the party, and many may love your jokes. But humour is primarily due to personality, appearance, and timing. If you take all this away and write down the joke instead, it loses all the supporting performance and may appear tasteless or even offensive, although if you told it face-to-face it would have been acceptable. Attempts at humour are not restricted to jokes; asides or comments which you think are funny are just as bad. Don't be tempted to use any of them in written form.

Sarcasm

Never use sarcasm. It does not work – again because it is a form of humour, albeit savage, and requires your facial expression and demeanour to make it work. A sarcastic comment in a letter could be taken literally by someone who misunderstands. For example, 'You spend so much time telling us what to do, we're thinking about giving you the manager's job.'

Personal remarks

Never write personal, suggestive, provocative or sexy remarks or comments. You may have a very good relationship with one of your supervisors but you should never put such a remark in writing. While the person concerned may not take offence, they may not be the only person who reads it. Their work colleagues could read it or, if they take work home, a member of their family may read it and not appreciate its content.

Discriminatory remarks

Never write racist, sexist or ageist remarks or comments. You may think it humorous to write something like:

'I wish the company football team all the best for the match on Saturday. The sales team and I will be there to support you, but I don't expect the girls will come along because it will be cold and wet and it will mess up their hair. So we can all go for a pint afterwards unencumbered to celebrate your victory.'

Undoubtedly some of the female staff would not find this funny at all. Similarly, it may be an in-joke on the factory that most of the workforce on the shop-floor would laugh and joke about, but circulating a memo saying 'Anyone who is not Irish can consult the company doctor on any matter, including family planning' may be a joke too far that backfires nastily. In fact, even verbally repeating offensive statements like this can cause you to be charged under the laws preventing racial, sexual or other discrimination.

Politics and religion
Never mention religion or politics in letters. This is another area where offence is easily given, and you may well be accused of bigotry or worse.

Privacy
Always respect every employee's privacy. Never reveal personal details about anyone in any form of communication that could be read by someone else. If you were told in confidence by the personnel department about an employee's personal problems, it would be a disaster if you decided to write to that person and mention these problems, however well-meaning your letter. Even when an employee has told you what appears to be good news, for example, they are expecting a baby, or have recovered from a bad illness, it is their prerogative when to tell others, not yours.

Respect the law

Books detailing the various laws of employment would fill many bookshelves. There are numerous individual laws, all of which add up to this: an employee has many rights and you as their employer must be aware of these and respect them.

If you are a manager, you should be familiar with employment law affecting your business and employees, because it impinges on every part of your working life. If you are still trying to grasp the essentials, follow this basic principle that just about covers you for everything:

Whatever you or your company does or says to an employee should always be backed up, as quickly as possible, with a written statement to that effect so that there is no misunderstanding over what has happened, is going to happen or might happen.

There are strict rules for certain areas of business, such as sacking unsatisfactory employees; the dismissals procedure is well-defined and requires plenty of written evidence (in case your employee should take you to a tribunal) to record what has happened and what action you have taken. To be safe, everything – from the time you offer someone a job to the time they leave – should be documented.

Let's look at an example.

A prospective employee, Fred Jones, comes to you for an interview, and is the best candidate.

You offer Fred the job	This offer, in writing, must contain a complete job description, details of salary, working hours, and terms and conditions.
Fred accepts the job	You must produce a written contract of employment within a specified time. This must detail everything you have agreed with the new employee, and must be signed by them upon acceptance.
You change Fred's responsibilities	You will talk to Fred first of course, but such a change requires you to issue a detailed job description, almost like a job offer. Fred may choose to protest the changes, which he must do both verbally and in writing. If Fred accepts, he should let you know in writing.
You raise Fred's salary	This must also be in writing, and be copied to the relevant payments department.
You warn Fred of unsatisfactory work or behaviour	The first warning is verbal; the next two are written but preceded by verbal confirmation that written warning is being issued. Dismissal has to be written and as detailed as possible.
You make Fred redundant or offer him early retirement	Again, an initial face-to-face discussion is required, but such offers must be presented in writing, and must contain certain terms laid down by law.

There are of course many other situations that could occur, but we cannot cover them all; the list would be too long. It will suffice to say that all of these situations should be documented. If in doubt, it is always best to write it down.

In summary, written communications to employees require thought and care. They are documents of record that can be used against you with powerful effect if you do not exercise care when putting pen to paper. If in doubt, you should consult an expert in employment law.

Examples of letters from employer to employee

Below are a few examples showing how to respond to specific situations. There are of course many other situations that are not covered here.

Responding to job applicants

Borset Coast Path Project
St Georges House
St Georges Street
Borchester
BO3 6AA

(Date)

(Recipient's name and address)

Dear

Thank you for your application for the post of Information Officer on the Borset Coast Path Project. We have had many applications for this post so I am afraid it will take us some time to sort through them all. However, I would hope that we will be in contact with you again in two or three weeks.

Yours faithfully

Richard Gittins
Project Director

Requesting applicant to attend an interview

Jones, Smith, Brown & Brown
Commercial Chambers
12 King's Road
FARLEIGH
Hants
SB1 4DD

20 October 2000

Mr M Cox
15 Lindhurst Gardens
OLD POLESFORD
Hants
SL6 8RY

Dear Mr Cox

My partners and I were most interested in your application for the position of Litigation Solicitor at these offices.

We would like to meet you to discuss the position further, and I would therefore be glad if you would telephone my secretary to arrange an appointment as soon as possible.

Yours sincerely
Messrs Jones, Smith, Brown & Brown

Michael Jones

Offering employment

Jones, Smith, Brown & Brown
12 King's Road
FARLEIGH
Hants
ISB 4DD

4 November 2000

Mr M Cox
15 Lindhurst Gardens
OLD POLESFORD
Hants
SL6 8RY

Dear Mr Cox

I am delighted to tell you that my partners and I have decided to offer you the post of Litigation Solicitor with our firm.

Since you told me that you must give one month's notice to your present employers, it would seem sensible for you not to take up your position here until 2 January next. I have entered this date on the enclosed contract of employment, which I would ask you to sign and return to me as soon as possible.

I hope you will enjoy working at Jones, Smith, Brown & Brown.

Yours sincerely
Jones, Smith, Brown & Brown

Michael Jones
Enc.

Offering promotion

T Fender Ltd
The Industrial Estate
BALNEY
Herts
SA40 3UW

12 July 2000
Mrs E Scrape
3 Oldfield Road
TRING
Herts
TR9 7FS

Dear Elizabeth,
Further to our recent meeting, I am pleased to confirm your new appointment as head of our Personnel division. Please accept the congratulations of both myself and the managing director, as we wish you well with your new position.
You will be pleased to learn that Jane Sugarman has agreed to work as your personal assistant, and will be arranging the removal of your furniture and effects to your new office at the end of next week. Please let her know of any special requirements as soon as possible.
In the next few days, you will receive full details of your new responsibilities, and will be issued with a new job description and amended salary advice. If you wish to discuss any of these further, or if you have any questions, please do not hesitate to contact me.
Yours sincerely
For T Fender Ltd

Tom Fender
Director

This letter would be preceded by a face-to-face meeting in which the employee would be told of his or her success at obtaining the new position. This letter merely represents the formalisation of the process, before any new terms and conditions and a new job description are issued.

This letter could be adapted for use to congratulate a new employee on obtaining a position.

Accepting resignation

Creen & Sons Ltd
25 Weldon Road
LEEDS
LE1 8NM

1 October 2000

Mr Frank Rane
4 Oak Road
ALSOP
Yorks
NO7 3SD

Dear Frank

Thank you for your letter of 29 September resigning your employment with the company, which I accept with reluctance.

Your new position seems to be an excellent opportunity, which you richly deserve. I am only sorry that the company cannot offer you anything comparable at the present time.

I am grateful for the initiative and enthusiasm that you have brought to your job over the past five years and wish you every success in the future.

Yours sincerely

David Hobbis

Warning to an employee

The next letter shows the first step in trying to resolve unacceptable behaviour in an employee. It is an unofficial warning, not a formal part of the dismissal procedure.

Sales and Marketing Limited
Langdon House
Ship Street
READING
Berkshire
DT6 8UH

16 August 2000

Mr Brian Coulsden
12 Tree Drive
Oakley
READING
Berks
LY9 7UN

Dear Mr Coulsden,

I am afraid that I must write to you concerning your persistent late arrival at this office. It has not gone unnoticed, and if it continues I shall be forced to take the matter to higher authority.

If you have any problem which has a bearing on this matter, please do not hesitate to come and talk to me about it. I am sure we would both prefer a solution that did not involve disciplinary action.

Yours sincerely
Sales and Marketing Limited

Peter Garton
Personnel Manager

Giving notice of dismissal

Between sending the letter of warning and a dismissal letter such as that shown below would be several intermediate steps, including the first official written warning, one or more further written warnings, and a final written warning – which would be worded similarly to that below, stating that it was a 'final warning' so that the employee could not claim that he had received inadequate warning about his conduct. The letter below represents the final step if the situation has not been resolved meantime.

Universal Products Ltd
SOUTHWICK
Surrey
NF3 6JP

28 March 2000

Mr D Bull
1 Bracken Close
SOUTHWICK
Surrey
NF6 7EW

Dear Mr Bull

I very much regret having to write this letter. However, despite numerous verbal and two written warnings you have continued to arrive late at work. In addition, you have been insolent to your department manager Mr Davies on a number of occasions when he has reminded you about your timekeeping.

The company feels that you have been given sufficient time to mend your ways or to sort out any problems you may have had relating to this, and I am afraid I now have no alternative but to give you four weeks' notice of termination of employment with this company.

Yours sincerely

N Chatterton
Personnel Manager

Expressing condolence to an employee

This example deals with the delicate problem of how to respond to a death in the family of an employee. It is equally suitable whether you knew the deceased or not. This can be among the most difficult of letters to write, for obvious reasons. There is no need to dwell on the illness or death which may be the subject of your letter, although your letter should, of course, convey the sympathy which is intended. Letters should normally be brief and to the point. Always address the recipient by first name, even if this is not how you would normally address them at work.

Crane Co. Ltd
48 Bridge Lane
CROXFORD
Lancs
LA5 4PD

25 September 2000

Ms C Brown
2 Creek Avenue
FORSHAM
Lancs
LA5 9CV

Dear Carol

I was very sorry to learn of your father's death. It must have been a terrible shock for you. I sympathize with you and all your family on your bereavement.

I look forward to seeing you again on 29 September, if you are able to conclude your father's affairs by then.

Yours sincerely

Craig Smith

Writing to prospective employers

When writing to a prospective employer, it is important to remember that your letter will be your ambassador. It will create an impression of you in the mind of the recipient, on the basis of which a decision will be made whether to pursue your application. You must write or type your letter neatly, laying it out according to the conventions described earlier. Include all relevant information, but avoid unnecessary details; remember that the person you are writing to is probably busy. Do not be afraid to let a little of your character show through in your letter, but try not to be too informal or chatty.

If you are applying for a post that includes keyboard skills, your letter should be a perfect reflection of your skills. In some cases, employers are very impressed by a neatly handwritten letter, as it is such a rarity nowadays. If you know that the job you are applying for will involve a lot of handwriting (filling in forms by hand perhaps), opt for the handwritten letter to show the prospective employer that your handwriting is legible.

Applying for a job 'on spec'

You may occasionally need or want to write to an employer offering your services for a job that has not been advertised – applying 'on spec'. This often applies when first leaving school, further or higher education, or if you are made redundant. In this type of letter you must make an extra effort to convey a good impression; the reader is not necessarily looking for someone to employ and has to be persuaded that you are worthwhile.

Speak of your own abilities, qualifications and experience, and say why you think these would be useful to the organisation. If you are willing and able to do various jobs, make this clear; but never try to impress by claiming to be able to do things that you cannot manage or for which you are not qualified. State what jobs you think you can handle and at what level.

It is good practice to find out something about the organisation to which you are writing and then use what you have discovered in your letter, to show that you have taken some trouble. If possible, find out the name of the personnel manager or staff manager and write to him or her in person.

An example of a letter sent 'on spec' is shown in the section *Examples of letters to potential employers*.

Your curriculum vitae

It is beyond the scope of this book to tell you in detail how or how not to write your curriculum vitae (CV). There are many books on the subject, and many individuals and companies who offer to do the job for you. These may or may not be useful but you should always try to:

Be concise	Don't go into detail of everyday tasks, a list of responsibilities for each job will suffice.
Be honest	Don't claim responsibilities that are not yours, or qualifications you haven't got.
Be clear	Write in good, grammatical English and lay the details out sequentially.
Be basic	Don't use fancy fonts and coloured paper to attract attention – they don't, instead they look cheap and unprofessional.
Be relevant	Don't detail jobs you did ten years ago that are unrelated to your field of expertise; mention them only briefly, if at all.
Be professional	Don't use chatty, vogue words and don't try to impress with jargon. Mention hobbies and interests, your family and your expected salary in the briefest detail, if at all.
Be positive	Accentuate the good points; never say you left a job because it was boring, instead say you wanted more variety.

Accepting or rejecting a job offer

If you are successful and the job is offered to you, you should always request details in writing, and await the full details before responding. You may find that the job is ideal for you, or you may find some of the terms and conditions unacceptable. If there are issues you need to discuss, this can be done verbally, but any amendment to the issued terms must also be issued in writing, and countersigned by the employer and yourself.

If you do not want the position, or cannot agree on acceptable terms, refuse the position politely, explaining briefly why you are unable to accept it and thanking the employer for their time and consideration.

Examples of letters to potential employers

Following are a few examples of letters written to apply for jobs, then examples of how to accept or reject a job offer.

Applying for a job 'on spec'

Below is an example of a letter written to seek work, when none has been advertised.

18 Field Gardens
BRIMTON
Beds
AB6 5PR

7 February 2000

Mr M Davies
Staff Manager
J Bloggs & Sons Ltd
BRIMTON
Beds
MB4 PQ8

Dear Mr Davies

I am writing to enquire whether you have any vacancies for a junior office assistant.

I left King Edward's School last Christmas, having passed GCSE Examinations in English Language, Geography and French. In my last year at school I also took a course in typing and general office procedures, and I am keen to make proper use of these skills.

Since leaving school I have not been able to find a regular job, but I have done some temporary work with Messrs Smith and Jones, who have been pleased with my work. Mr Smith will be quite willing to give me a reference.

I realise that you may not have any vacancies at present, but I would be very willing to work in any department and to undertake any training required. I therefore hope that you will consider my application favourably whenever a possible position arises.

Yours sincerely

Caroline Brown (Miss)

Applying for job details

Below is an example of a letter requesting further details and a job application form:

> 15 Oakfield Drive
> CARTOWN
> Hampshire
> L12 7RT
>
> 15th January 2000
>
> The Secretary
> The Empire Trading Company
> Ships Wharf
> BRIARLEY
> Hampshire
> SO5 7RX
>
> Dear Sir
>
> In reply to your advertisement for an Export Manager in The Echo (9th January 2000), I would be grateful if you would send me an application form and further details of the position.
>
> Yours faithfully
>
> Frank Binns

Applying for the job

Always remember to be brief and courteous; provide relevant information but leave the detail for the curriculum vitae, if you send one, or for the interview, if not.

Below are two examples of letters written to apply for a job. In the first, the applicant does not include a curriculum vitae.

55 Davidson Avenue
MANCHTER
FP7 7TS

21st January 2000

Mr H Ody
The Apsley Motor Company
Jowett Road
MANCHTER
MN3 IAK

Dear Mr Ody

I wish to apply for the position of skilled motor mechanic as advertised in today's Manchter Gazette.

Having completed a full apprenticeship, I have been employed by Jones Motors in the London Road for the past two years. I am now anxious to move to a firm where there are greater prospects for promotion and more interesting and varied work.

My present manager, Mr Brian, has agreed to give me a reference, and I would be free to attend an interview any evening after 4.30 p.m.

Yours sincerely,

John Collins

The above letter illustrates that it is a good idea, if you are already in a job, to explain why you are leaving in case anyone thinks you are being asked to leave.

The next letter is an example of one you could send to accompany your curriculum vitae.

Hollydene
Collingwood Road
NANTON
Beds
SL5 6XC

1st February 2000

Box 3998
The Daily Mercury
156 Hope Lane
LONDON
EC3 7YP

Dear Sirs,

I am writing in answer to your advertisement in today's Daily Mercury for a Sales Representative.

I have had seven years' experience of the type of selling you outline, starting as a trainee with ILC Ltd, and progressing to my present position of Area Sales Representative (South-East) with Jones Brothers of Dunstable. I am now keen to advance my career in a larger organisation with opportunities to engage in overseas selling techniques.

I enclose my curriculum vitae, including the names of two referees. If you think I may be suitable for this position, I should be happy to come for an interview at any time convenient to you.

Yours faithfully,

Colin Brown

Enc.

There is no need to go into great detail about your work experience and qualifications as your curriculum vitae will cover all of that.

Accepting a job offer

Hollydene
Collingwood Road
NANTON
Beds
SL5 6XC

15 October 2000

R Burns Esq
Personnel Manager
Timetec Limited
Rose Estate
OXRIDGE
Bucks
SL9 5RF

Dear Mr Burns

Thank you very much for your letter of 12 October offering me the position of Sales Representative with your company.

I am delighted to accept the position, and look forward to starting work with you on 13 November.

Yours sincerely

Miss J Alcock

Rejecting a job offer

Hollydene
Collingwood Road
NANTON
Beds
SL5 6XC

15 October 2000

R Burns Esq
Personnel Manager
Timetec Limited
Rose Estate
OXRIDGE
Bucks
SL9 5RF

Dear Mr Burns

Thank you very much for your letter of 12 October offering me the position of Sales Representative with your company.

However, I regretfully have to decline as I have been offered, and have accepted, a similar position with a company that is much closer to my home. I am sure you understand that, as I have a young family, I wish to spend as much time with them as work commitments will allow and reducing my travelling time will help considerably.

Thank you once again for offering me the position, and for your confidence in my abilities. I am sure that a company with a reputation such as yours will have no difficulty in finding another candidate for the job.

Yours sincerely

Miss J Alcock

Writing to your existing employer

There are several situations in which you may need to write to your employer. Some examples are:

- When requesting certain types of statutory leave, such as maternity or paternity leave, or non-statutory leave such as an unpaid period of additional holiday
- When requesting a transfer to another department, or promotion
- When requesting a reference for another job
- When handing in your notice.

Let us look at each of these in detail.

Requesting leave

In many cases it is not necessary to write to your employer requesting leave. You may be told when you have to take your holidays, for example, or it may be arranged on a rota basis. Similarly, if you are sick for a day or two, or if you have an emergency, it would be silly to expect you to make time to write a letter explaining why, when a telephone call or fax would do. Most employers are quite reasonable in this respect.

However, there are certain types of leave for which written notice must be given, generally where there is a need for you or the employer to apply for statutory benefits, such as maternity pay or extended sickness pay. Such letters should contain all relevant information and nothing more. For example, in the case of a maternity claim, you must state the date on which the baby is expected to arrive, the date you intend to leave work, and the date you intend to return (if you do); there is no need to tell your employer additional details such as the names you have chosen for your baby or the arrangements you are making for childcare.

Examples of several types of leave request are shown at the end of this section.

Requesting promotion or a transfer

It is not always easy to write a letter asking your boss to promote you. You may think that he will laugh at you, or will think you are being presumptuous. However, in the right situation, a little self-promotion goes a long way. There is rarely any harm in putting yourself forward for a job you know you can do – particularly if you know that the job is becoming vacant, and is due to be advertised – as long as you do not take the possibility of rejection as a personal insult. There may be valid reasons why someone else is more suitable for the job, so don't be too disappointed if you don't get the job you want.

In such circumstances it is preferable to address your letter directly to the manager of the relevant department, rather than to the Personnel department. An example is shown at the end of this section.

Requesting a reference

When applying for a job, you are often asked to provide written references, or the names of one or more 'referees' to whom the company can apply for an opinion on your experience, your character, and your suitability for the position.

When applying for a new position with your current employer you are not usually required to provide references, but it always helps if your request for a transfer, promotion, or other move within a company is supported by your immediate manager, or another higher in the management chain.

There may be other reasons why you would ask for a reference from your employer: when obtaining personal credit from a financial institution, for example, you may be required to provide written evidence of your current salary, and any prospects for promotion. Similarly, certain clubs, societies and trade organisations may require personal or business references or recommendations.

Examples of requests for references are given at the end of this section; example references are shown in the section *Other letters relating to employment*.

Resignation letters and letters of refusal

If you decide to resign your position, or refuse an offer of transfer or promotion, you should first seek out the appropriate manager for a face-to-face discussion. After this, however, if you are still determined to proceed, you should put the details in writing, including your reasons and a date where appropriate. Be firm and polite and try to inject some positivity into the letter, by thanking the company for the offer (if refusing an offer) or by mentioning how you have enjoyed or benefited from working for them.

An example resignation letter is shown on page 152; an acceptance of resignation is provided on page 130.

Writing a letter of complaint

Usually most complaints within the workplace can be dealt with face-to-face, but occasionally if nothing is done to rectify a situation, you will need to resort to a written communication. Do not be afraid to take up issues with your employer, particularly those regarding health and safety or the rights of employees. There are laws to protect you in the event of a dispute. If you are a member of a trade union, it is often preferable to bring the matter to their attention, rather than dealing with it alone: others may have the same complaint. If you are not in a trade union, ask your colleagues about the problem and see if you can get them to support you: a letter written by a number of employees may carry more weight than a single complaint.

On page 153, you will find a sample letter of complaint dealing with breaches of health and safety codes regarding workplace facilities.

Examples of letters to existing employers

In this section we provide sample letters covering a variety of situations in which you may need to write to your employer.

Requesting leave

Here are three examples of letters written to an employer requesting leave, each for a different but valid reason.

The first letter is a request for unpaid compassionate leave to look after a sick relative.

4 Farren Road
LONDON
SE6 8UH

2 July 2000

Mr Nichols
Sales Manager
Grant & Sons Ltd
19 Church Lane
LONDON
SE4 91G

Dear Mr Nichols

I would be grateful to receive your permission for me to be absent from work next week (8-12 July).

I am needed to look after my mother, who is an invalid, during this week. The carer who normally looks after her is required urgently elsewhere next week, and at such short notice, I have been unable to arrange alternative care. This is an exceptional situation, which I do not anticipate recurring.

I hope that you will give my request sympathetic consideration. I appreciate that I would not be paid for this week.

Yours sincerely

Jane Ryman

Many employers would be happy to authorise such leave on the basis of a verbal request, but it is always best to provide a written request, and request a written answer, in case of any future dispute over the matter. This particularly applies if you are entitled to a certain amount of paid compassionate leave.

The next example is a letter excusing absence from work because of the writer's own illness.

15 Greenland Road
SAMPTER
Essex
ES3 8UJ

3 December 2000

Mr H Jones
Head of Sales Department
Hampton & Co Ltd
12-14 High Street
SAMPTER
Essex
ES7 4ED

Dear Mr Jones

I left a telephone message with your secretary this morning to explain that I was feeling unwell, and was going to visit my doctor.

He has diagnosed an infection of the respiratory tract, and suggested I would probably need to be off work for at least ten days. I enclose a medical certificate.

I have spoken to John Griffiths about my work commitments for the next few days and I believe that things are under control, but if anybody has any problems about my work they should not hesitate to telephone me.

Yours sincerely

Gerald Long

Enc.

It is generally deemed unnecessary these days to write to an employer regarding your illness unless you are likely to be absent for some time – say more than seven days. Some may not require it at all. As you generally have to supply a medical certificate for absences over this period, however, a letter to accompany it is usually welcome, and provides evidence in the case of any dispute over notification.

The next letter is rarely required by an employer – most are too tactful to request one – but in the circumstances, many people find it easier to write than to telephone with such news. This letter excuses the writer's absence from work because of the death of a close relative.

> 2 Creek Avenue
> FORSHAM
> Lancs
> LA5 9CV
>
> 23 September 2000
>
> Dear Mr Smith
>
> I regret that I was not at work today and will be unable to attend for the rest of the week. My father died suddenly yesterday evening and I am needed here to help settle his affairs and to make arrangements for the funeral. Also, the whole family, including myself, are very shaken by his death.
>
> I expect to be back at work on Monday 29 September.
>
> Yours sincerely
>
> Carol Brown

In letters like this – which verge on the personal – the recipient's address can be omitted. A suggested response to such a letter by the employer is shown in the section *Examples of letters from employer to employee*.

Enquiring about promotion prospects

Here is a typical example.

2 Hornsby Terrace
UPTON
Surrey
SU8 3WE

5 June 2000

Ms K Tope
Accounts Manager
Smith & Co. Ltd
54-58 Pine Road
UPTON
Surrey
SU4 5RF

Dear Ms Tope

I am writing to ask whether you would consider promoting me to the position of Senior Clerk.

As you know, I have been working for the company for four years, one year as Junior Clerk and three years as Clerk. I have undertaken the work of Senior Clerk during periods of holiday and sickness and, apart from finding the work very interesting, I believe that I have performed it satisfactorily. I have a number of ideas for improving the efficiency of the Department, which the scope of my present job does not allow me to implement.

I would be grateful for the opportunity to discuss this matter.

Yours sincerely

Robert Smith

Requesting an internal transfer

Here is an example of how to broach the subject of an inter-company transfer.

Laboratory B5

3 April 2000

Mr H Green
Personnel Manager
Block H

Dear Mr Green

I am writing to request a transfer to laboratory B1. There are two principal reasons for this request.

Firstly, I am particularly interested in some of the problems on which this laboratory plans to initiate research. Secondly, a personality clash has arisen over the past few months within my own department, which I find very disturbing. I have, otherwise, been very happy during my three years of employment here.

I feel that my knowledge and experience would be equally well suited to the work in laboratory B1. The project I have been working on for the past year should be completed in a month and it would create the minimum disturbance if I transferred then.

I hope that you will give this matter your favourable consideration.

Yours sincerely

Jane White

Requesting a reference

In many cases, you may prefer to ask a previous employer for a reference when applying for a job, rather than your current employer. Here is an example of how to do so.

> 25 Oakley Avenue
> MILTON
> Northants
> SY12 4LT
>
> 14 May 2000
>
> Mr B Brown
> M & B Creative Marketing
> Dower House
> PORTON
> Northants
> RT6 3ER
>
> Dear Mr Brown
>
> I am applying for the post of Salesman with Kingley Marketing of Milton, and I wondered whether you would be willing for me to give your name as a referee.
>
> I have been very happy in my present post, as I was during my four years with M & B, but I have decided to apply for the post with Kingley Marketing as it seems to offer greater responsibility and a chance to use my own initiative more frequently.
>
> Please pass on my regards to any of my colleagues still with M & B and, of course, to Mrs Brown.
>
> Yours sincerely
>
> Brian Butts

Requesting a character reference

If you are applying for, say, a mortgage, you may be asked to provide a reference from your employer to prove your income, the likelihood of continued employment, and any prospects for promotion. It is wise to request such a reference in writing, so you can show the bank you have requested it.

> 4 Rose Wood
> OXRIDGE
> Bucks
> SL5 6XC
>
> 15 February 2000
>
> Mr Fred Jones
> Projects Director
> Timetec Limited
> OXRIDGE
> Bucks SL9 5RF
>
> Dear Mr Jones
>
> I am applying for a mortgage from Big Bank, and I wondered whether, as a senior representative of my employer, you would provide me with a written reference to support my application.
>
> Such a reference would contain details of my current position and my recent promotions, current salary and future salary expectations, and an assessment of my character. The reference should be sent directly to the bank at the address shown below, quoting the reference shown.
>
> If you are unable to do this, would you please let me know so I can ask someone else.
>
> Yours sincerely
>
> Mrs J Godsell
>
> Bank address: Big Bank
> 30 High Street
> OXRIDGE
> SL9 3HY
> Please quote ref: M293726/JWG.

Resigning your position

The following letter could be adapted for most situations. If you have not been happy in your employment, you may want to omit the last two paragraphs.

4 Oak Road
Creigh
ALSOP
Yorks
NO7 3SD

29 September 2000

Mr D Hobbis
Sales Manager
Creen & Sons Ltd
25 Weldon Road
LEEDS
LE1 8NM

Dear Mr Hobbis

I have been offered, and have decided to accept, the position of Sales Manager with Broom & Sons Ltd. I am writing, therefore, to give you the appropriate four weeks' notice to terminate my employment with the Company on 27 October.

I have been very happy during my five years here and it was with some sorrow that I reached this decision. However, my new position offers considerably more scope and responsibility than my present one.

I would like to take this opportunity to thank you for all the support and guidance you have given me over the past five years.

Yours sincerely

Frank Rane

Complaining to your employer

In this letter, the writer is complaining constructively about a health and safety issue, on behalf of himself and his colleagues. If you are in a union, you may wish to write to them, or send them a copy of the letter, in such a circumstance.

Accounts Department
Third Floor
6 February 2000

Ms D Kenny
Personnel Manager
Fifth Floor

Dear Ms Kenny

I wish to draw your attention to the washing facilities on the third floor. Only one sink is provided for over one hundred male employees on this floor. There is usually neither soap nor clean towels available.

This must be detrimental to the health of employees and is certainly a waste of the Company's money since much work time is lost in queuing for the use of these inadequate facilities. I believe this, in fact, to be in contravention of the laws relating to Heath and Safety At Work.

I would be grateful if you would look into this matter urgently, with a view to providing adequate, well-maintained facilities.

Yours sincerely

On behalf of the Accounts Department
John Harris

Other letters related to employment

The following letters concern employers and potential or past employees, but are not directly from one to the other.

Taking up a reference

Kingsley Marketing
64 King Street
MILTON
Northants
SY7 8PL
23 May 2000

B Brown Esq
M & B Creative Marketing
Dower House
PORTON
Northants
RT6 3ER

Dear Mr Brown

Mr Brian Butts, of 25 Oakley Avenue, Milton, has applied to me for the post of Salesman. I understand that he was employed by you for four years in a similar capacity.

He has put your name forward as a referee, and I would be most grateful if you would let me know whether you found him capable and totally reliable. I am particularly concerned to know whether, in your experience, he is able to work independently on his own initiative.

It goes without saying that whatever you tell me will be treated in the strictest confidence.

I am enclosing a stamped addressed envelope for your reply.

Yours sincerely
Kingsley Marketing

John George

Providing a reference (personal)

Timetec Limited
OXRIDGE
Bucks
SL9 5RF
Your ref: M293726/JWG.

15 February 2000
Big Bank
30 High Street
OXRIDGE
Bucks
SL9 3HY

Dear Sirs

I have been asked by Mrs Jane Godsell to provide a reference regarding her character and her position with my company.

Jane has worked for Timetec for almost eight years, and during this time has proved a asset to the workforce. She excels at organisation, and has been promoted several times since starting in our production department. She now works directly for the Marketing Manager and is responsible for our promotions budget and much of our marketing effort. She has agreed to take on the Manager's job to cover maternity leave later this year, and should the position later fall vacant, Jane would be our first choice as replacement.

Her current salary is £21,725 per annum, plus bonuses, which average £3,000 over the past two years. As Marketing Manager, both salary and bonuses would increase by approximately 20%, and she will be paid at this higher rate throughout her appointment.

If you require any further information, please contact me personally at the above address.

Yours sincerely

F W Jones
Projects Director

Providing a reference (business)

Timber Products Limited
MILBORNE
Dorset
YT7 91J

Your ref PR7/8/82
Our ref MD/JL

30 August 2000
CONFIDENTIAL

The Personnel Manager
Royal Oak Timber Company
MARKYATE
Dorset
RT6 90K

Dear Sir

In reply to your request for information about James Long, who has applied for the position of Works Manager with your company, I can confirm he has been an employee at this company for 8 years.

He served a two-year apprenticeship with us, and a year later was promoted to Line Foreman. He has always shown himself to be a hard worker and is a popular and helpful member of our workforce. Last year we put his managerial skills to the test with promotion to Assistant Works Manager, and we found our decision to be fully justified.

Mr Long is an honest and reliable person and has, I believe, the initiative, experience and capabilities to handle the job for which he has applied.

If you require any further information, please do not hesitate to get in touch with me.

Yours faithfully
Royal Oak Timber Company

Michael Deacon
Managing Director

CHAPTER 13

Awkward letters

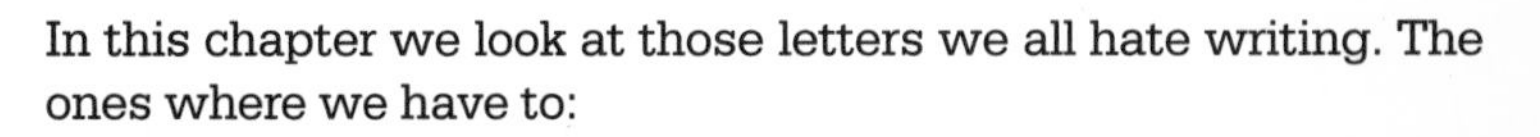

In this chapter we look at those letters we all hate writing. The ones where we have to:

- apologise for our mistakes
- chase debts
- complain about something
- threaten legal action
- deal with awkward customers or suppliers
- refuse something.

We may not like them, but they all have to be done. We look at the best way to write these letters effectively, and include some samples on which you can base your own letters. Some of these are from one business to another; others between business and individual. Many can be easily adapted for use in personal business, such as the letters between landlord and tenant or business and debtor.

General guidelines for awkward letters

The main advice when writing an 'awkward letter' is to be dispassionate about it: trying to inject a lot of emotion into a letter doesn't really work; it simply portrays you as a petty person and does not relay the truth of the situation. It is best to be calm and not to use inflammatory language in these letters. Some words are really too strong and should be toned down for the purposes of a letter.

For example:

Instead of ...	*Try ...*
I am disgusted	I am dismayed
I am horrified	I am taken aback
We are worried	We are concerned
The MD is furious	The MD is not pleased
Your product is rubbish	Your product is inferior
You've made no effort	You could try harder
The figures are laughable	The figures are not what I expected

You may consider these to be rather inferior alternatives, and feel that you need to be more direct in your criticism. However, always bear in mind that there could be further action required on the matter at a later date; a lengthy wrangle over unpaid money or broken contracts, for example, which could involve litigation. If so, and you are seen to have been more than reasonable, you will be at an advantage. Then you will have the opportunity to say what you really feel! However, opening correspondence on a subject with confrontational or aggressive language is excessive, and will simply give the other party reason to be obstinate.

Apologising to customers

There is one exception to the advice above, and that is the written apology. In this instance, use whatever emotive language you need to in order to convey how sorry you are. Many companies really do grovel when they are apologising to an important customer or client whose business they really value and are scared of losing, but when it comes to apologising to the faceless members of the public these same companies are often dismissive. This is a shame because if they are in the business of selling products or services to the public then they should treat each customer as important. Here is your chance to improve your company's policy.

In the chapter *Making a start,* you will find a list of suggested openings for letters of apology. As stated in that chapter, it is important to get the important emotion in the first line. Do not leave it until later in the letter, or your letter could be thrown away by a disgusted customer who thinks that all you are going to do for the whole of the letter is make excuses. Here is an example of a *badly* structured letter of apology, which would not help matters at all.

> John Martin & Sons Ltd
> Grendle Farm
> Cattle Drive
> Somerfield
> SN9 OPP
>
> 12th January 2000
>
> Mr John Smith
> The Old Mill
> River Stream Road
> Wandle
> W8Q 8NN
>
> Dear Sir,
>
> Re: Late delivery of goods
>
> We understand that you have complained that you have not received your usual weekly supply of cattle feed from us. I note from your records that we usually deliver to you on Mondays but that, due to our driver being taken ill on the Sunday, the relief driver was not able to get to you until Tuesday morning. It was not possible to telephone all our customers to tell them what was happening and, anyway, most people received their usual delivery on the usual day. Only a few people had to wait another 24 hours.
>
> We apologise for any inconvenience.
>
> Yours sincerely,
>
> John Martin

This letter is full of excuses and shows no consideration for the actual inconvenience caused to the customer, even though the word 'inconvenience' is used. There is no reassurance in the letter that the error will not happen again, nor is there any real apology or expression of the customer's value. The following is a better example of how such a letter should be framed:

John Martin & Sons Ltd
Grendle Farm
Cattle Drive
Somerfield
SN9 OPP

12th January 2000

Mr John Smith
The Old Mill
River Stream Road
Wandle
W8Q 8NN

Dear Sir,

Re: Late delivery of goods

May I sincerely apologise for the inconvenience caused to you by the late delivery of your cattle feed last week. This was due to unfortunate and unforeseen circumstances – namely, the regular driver was taken ill the day before he usually makes your delivery – and poor communication – the relief driver did not inform us at that he would be unable to deliver to all our regular customers by the end of Monday and would be completing the round the following morning.

Had we known this in time, we would have telephoned you to explain the problem. Should this situation arise again, we will be better prepared.

Once again, please accept our apologies for the late delivery and please be assured that you are one of our most valued customers.

Yours sincerely,

John Martin

The second letter is very much better and almost makes the reader feel sorry for the person who is apologising. There is one point, however, that has not been mentioned so far and is of inestimable value when writing an apology. Apologise before the customer complains. If you can act quickly to show that you have recognised your error before anyone else has had time to complain, it is a good plus point.

Chasing debts

One of the most tedious and frustrating jobs of the business letter writer is writing to prompt or demand payment of an outstanding debt. The following points may help you if you have to write such a letter:

- Letters concerning money matters should always be written in a clear and precise manner. It is best to avoid archaic phrases which your reader might misunderstand, and to write in concise sentences that leave no possibility of ambiguity.
- When writing letters to a company or financial institution it is best to address a particular individual. If you cannot find out the name of the appropriate person, at least make sure that your letter is addressed to the correct department.
- Never be rude, even if you are angry. State the subject matter of your letter in the first paragraph and follow through the other points you want to make in a logical order. By sticking entirely to the facts in this way, you will put your case with the least likelihood of misunderstanding or causing offence. Remember also that the letter may be used as evidence if the debt is recovered via a court procedure. Check your facts and do not make idle or ill-founded threats against the debtor, even in jest.
- It is often helpful to enclose relevant documents such as receipts. If you do this, always send copies, not originals, and say what you have enclosed in the text of your letter.
- Always quote any reference given to a letter to which you are replying. Even if you do not use references yourself, they will help your correspondent and thus speed up the handling of your business.

There are a number of documents used to prompt a debtor into payment. We will look at them in the order in which they should be issued.

Issuing a statement

This is the first line of attack. A statement is a reminder of the original invoice or invoices that have still not been paid. Below is an example of a statement:

AUTO MOTORS UK LIMITED STATEMENT

Please send payment direct to Accounts Office : 56 Ebury Street
MANCHESTER
LM8 6AT
Tel: 0161 989 456

Lewis Spares
6-8 West Road
HIGH WYCOMBE
Buckinghamshire
SL7 5RQ

11th February 2000

Date of sale	Reference	Amount
08/01/1999	42002 INV	27.95
15/01/1999	42069 INV	9.82
31/01/1999	42098 INV	3.40
05/02/1999	42121 INV	16.84
Balance outstanding		58.01

If your terms of payment are explicit and have been agreed to by the debtor (many companies print them on the back of order forms, for example), it is often worth printing them again at the bottom of such a statement; especially if you intend to charge interest on overdue payments.

Requesting settlement of an overdue account

If the statement has been ignored, the next step is to send a letter requesting that the account be settled. Again, there should be no threat. For example:

Napley Timber Limited
Walter's Yard
BROUGHTON
Sussex
LU7 5TN

6 February 2000
F Hunter Esq.
63 Westerham Road
BROUGHTON
Sussex
LU9 6TV

Dear Mr Hunter,

We refer to our previous invoices:
I9823_3x issued 12 October 1999
I9874_4f issued 30 November 1999
and our recent statement of account, issued 6 January 2000.

We would appreciate your immediate payment for the timber supplied to you during October and November 1999, as per these invoices.

We are now preparing our books for auditing and the delay in receiving your settlement is causing some inconvenience.

A duplicate statement is enclosed.

Yours sincerely,
Napley Timber Limited

Brian Kent

Issuing a final demand

The preceeding letter is quite a reasonable request: it 'asks' for settlement of outstanding bills. But it has been ignored, nevertheless. This next example 'demands' settlement and is more urgent. Here, in fact, a threat is included in the last paragraph.

Napley Timber Limited
Walter's Yard
BROUGHTON
Sussex
LU7 5TN

15 February 2000

F Hunter Esq.
63 Westerham Road
BROUGHTON
Sussex
LU9 6TV

Dear Mr Hunter

We regret to note that your account for timber supplied during October and November 1999 is still outstanding. We have now written to you on two occasions, enclosing a duplicate statement each time to serve as a reminder.

In these circumstances, I am afraid that unless we receive settlement within seven working days of the date of this letter I shall be forced to instruct our solicitors to take action.

Yours sincerely

Napley Timber Limited

Peter Harvey Limited
Managing Director

You will note from the above example that it is signed by a senior person in the company. The recipient of the letter will be much more impressed by the seriousness of the threat to take legal action if it comes from the person who is empowered to authorise such action. Also, note that you must give the bad payer a reasonable amount of time to respond to your letter (in the above example it is seven days) before you start legal proceedings.

A letter threatening legal proceedings should never be written unless you really feel that no other course remains open and you are prepared to carry out that threat. If circumstances do demand that such a letter be sent, it is sensible to send it by recorded delivery mail. Never make personal threats: keep it businesslike and polite.

Making a complaint

Complaining letters can portray you as a tedious moaner unless you get the balance right. In order for a complaint to be effective you have to use language which shows you are firm and businesslike – not irrational and hysterical. The facts of the complaint must be presented at the beginning of the letter and the request for action should follow. As with letters that you send to chase debts, letters of complaint may need to become more severe in tone if the first and second letters are not heeded. The following examples are of a business tenant to a landlord asking him to effect repairs.

Making an initial complaint

Holford and Duttine plc
The Bank Chambers
94 Court Road
POOLFORD
Dorset
JO9 5TB

5th February 2000
Ian Graham Esq.
40 Moreley Drive
POOLFORD
Dorset
JP8 6YB

Dear Mr Graham,

Re: Urgent repairs at the above address

During the last three days a large crack has developed in the ceiling of our main office. Pieces of plaster have fallen off and additional hairline cracks are appearing. I have been into the roof space and can find no dampness or other obvious cause of the problem.

I should be most grateful if you would arrange for a builder to inspect the property as soon as possible since I fear that even more serious damage may occur.

Yours sincerely,

Michael Duttine

The above is a perfectly reasonable request by a tenant for action to be taken by the owner of the building. If there is no response to this first letter then another, firmer letter may be sent.

Making a further request for action

Holford & Duttine plc
The Bank Chambers
94 Court Road
POOLFORD
Dorset
JO9 5TB

12th February 2000
Ian Graham Esq.
40 Moreley Drive
POOLFORD
Dorset
JP8 6YB

Dear Mr Graham,

Re: Outstanding urgent repairs

I am afraid that I must write to you again regarding the state of the ceiling in our main office. Further pieces of plaster have fallen off and the whole ceiling is covered in a fine network of cracks. I am very concerned about the safety of my staff and therefore I would appreciate your immediate attention in these matters.

Yours sincerely,

Michael Duttine

Issuing a letter of last resort

If the second letter produces no results and the situation is hazardous, unpleasant or unhygienic then you should take legal and/or local authority advice. For example, in the case of blocked drains, or other situations in which health and safety may be compromised, the local Environmental Health inspectorate can be called in to advise. The letter of last resort should be as follows:

Holford & Duttine plc
The Bank Chambers
94 Court Road
POOLFORD
Dorset
JO9 5TB

20th February 2000
Ian Graham Esq.
40 Moreley Drive
POOLFORD
Dorset
JP8 6YB

Dear Mr Graham,

Re: Outstanding urgent repairs

I refer to my letters dated the 5th and 12th of this month regarding the cracked and potentially dangerous ceiling in our main office. As I have received no response from you whatsoever, I have to inform you that I have taken legal advice in the matter. I was advised that, owing to the serious and urgent nature of the repair required, I should call in a builder immediately. I have done so and they are starting work tomorrow.

This work necessitates closing our offices for two days because of the hazardous nature of the repair work. Upon the advice of my solicitors, I will be presenting you with a bill in due course, which will cover all repair work and loss of income through the two-day closure of the office.

It is regrettable that you have not responded to any previous communications and that we should have to resort to taking legal action.

Yours sincerely

Michael Duttine

Obviously, should a complaint escalate in this way, do make sure you take proper legal advice before following such a course of action. Do not assume that you have the law on your side in any issue. The law, sadly, does not always agree.

Dealing with awkward people

Customers with justifiable complaints should be sent a gracious letter of apology as per the first section of this chapter. There are, however, people who seem to have nothing better to do than write niggling letters to companies, probably because they like to complain about everything. The best response if you receive such a letter is to be calm and polite.

Responding to an irrational complaint

In the first instance, you can respond personally, addressing the comments in the letter you have received:

Watkins & Co.
4 Manor Road
PLUMTREE
Norfolk
PL2 99Z

12th February 2000

Mr P Watts
19 Acacia Avenue
TOOTING
Manchester
MN1 6QQ

Dear Mr Watts,

Thank you for your letter of the 5th February 2000.

I am sorry that you find the colour of our delivery vans irritating but orange is our corporate colour and we find that customers associate our company with that particular colour scheme. It would be extremely expensive for us to respray all our vehicles, as I am sure you understand.

Thank you for your communication on this matter.

Yours sincerely,

Mr G Humbold
General Manager

Responding to continual irrational complaints

If the letters continue to arrive you can resort to a standard letter which is merely sent out to anyone who is sending your company irrational letters. It could be worded something like this:

Watkins & Co
Sandy Lodge
Manor Road
PLUMTREE
Norfolk
PL2 99Z

12th February 2000

Dear Sir/Madam,

Thank you for your letter.

We have noted your comments but cannot, at this time, change our working practices in the manner which you suggest.

Yours sincerely,

Mr G Humbold
General Manager

Note the lack of an address for the recipient. That way the awkward person gets the message that you have relegated him/her to a standard letter, and may desist from further communication.

If they do not give up, despite receiving only standard letters by way of reply, the only thing left to do is ignore their letters (having read them first, of course, to make sure that this complaint is not legitimate – even awkward people do occasionally have a legitimate complaint!).

Standard letters of the type shown above should never be sent to bonafide customers as they are a rather contemptuous way of corresponding with people.

Polite refusals

People in business are often asked to donate to charities, speak at functions or attend meetings, and may even be offered jobs they have not applied for (called 'headhunting'), but which circumstances dictate that they have to refuse. Such refusal should always be expressed in a tone of regret and the reason for refusal should always be fully explained. Some examples are shown below.

Refusing to donate funds

Watkins & Co.
4 Manor Road
PLUMTREE
Norfolk
PL2 99Z

18 October 2000

J Smith
The Society for Freedom of Office Workers
BLACKWELL
London
WH1 6QQ

Dear Mr Smith,

Thank you for your letter of 12 October requesting a donation for your charity.

Unfortunately, although we might wish to donate to all worthwhile charities that approach us, we do not have the funds and so it is company policy that each year we choose two charities to receive our allocated charitable donations.

We will, however, keep your letter on file and consider your organisation's needs when we have our annual charity fund meeting.

Thank you once again for writing to us.

Yours sincerely

Mr G Humbold
General Manager

Refusing to speak at a function

Holford & Duttine plc
The Bank Chambers
94 Court Road
POOLFORD
Dorset
JO9 5TB

12th February 2000

J Simpson
Allsorts Conference Planners
Conference House
Westwood
BIRMINGHAM
B34 3JF

Dear Ms Simpson

Thank you for your very flattering invitation to be one of your speakers at the annual trade conference next year.

However, I do not feel that I am the best expert on the topic that you suggest and that you could approach more qualified people in this area. May I suggest the following names?

J D Lovett, of Lovett & Partners, Tel: 028 8236123.
H Crankshaw, of Robert Fliddle & Co, Tel: 028 8236152.

Thank you for approaching me and it is with regret that I must decline the invitation but I feel sure that either of the above could be admirable alternatives.

Yours sincerely

Martha Duttine

Refusing to attend a meeting or event

Holford & Duttine plc
The Bank Chambers
94 Court Road
POOLFORD
Dorset
JO9 5TB

12 February 2000

John Fielding
Holford International plc
Holford House
LANCING
West Sussex
BG28 2IH

Dear John,

Thank you for your letter of 6 February suggesting a meeting next month in Paris.

I am afraid that I will be extremely busy next month on the preparation of a major design project for which our branch has been commissioned, and I am therefore not scheduling any meetings until this project is complete. I do hope that you understand.

Perhaps we can arrange another date?

I look forward to hearing from you.

Yours sincerely,

Martha Duttine

Refusing an unexpected job offer

12 Broughton Way
Woodleigh
BREMFORD
Bucks
SL7 5TX

12th February 2000
Mr Franco Angeloni
Goodstaff Recruitment Ltd
Staff House
HAMLEY
Bucks
SL3 7FH

Dear Mr Angeloni

Thank you for your offer of the position of Contracts Negotiator with your company. I was surprised and flattered to receive your invitation, as I had not applied directly to you for a position, nor spoken to you on the subject.

While your offer is certainly interesting, in fact I am happy with my current position, which has recently been extended to include exciting new responsibilities. I particularly wish to lead my team through to the end of the current project as I have given a commitment to do so. After this, if I decide it is time to change job, I may approach you to see if we can agree on a mutually acceptable position.

Meanwhile, many thanks for your considerate offer. I am sure you will have little difficulty in finding someone else to fill the position, and wish you all the best.

Yours sincerely

Michael Hanford

There are lots of awkward situations that crop up in business. We have just dealt with a few in this chapter. Just remember that any letter you send is a reflection of you and/or your company. If you try to be gracious, polite, reasonable, patient – and firm when necessary – it will reflect well and cause the least possible offence.

CHAPTER 14

Writing effective promotional material

In this chapter we look at promotional correspondence used to generate sales or advertise or market a product. This includes the press release, sales letter and many other documents. While this is not a marketing manual, and there are certainly many available that would be helpful in creating such correspondence, there are certain principles of layout, content and tone that it is apt to describe here.

Sales, marketing and PR through letters, e-mail and faxes is becoming harder and harder, mainly because people have become so inundated with junk mail that they rarely respond to or even read sales letters any more. However, promotional material that is properly targetted – sent to a named person whose needs have been established and who would probably be interested in the product or service – can pay dividends.

One of the main problems of bad promotional material is that it operates on a 'scatter-gun' approach. Such companies feel that if they send out enough sales literature to enough people a certain number of them will respond. Most marketing manuals will tell you that this is a waste of money and that you should narrow the target market down only to those groups of people who will be interested. In order to write effective promotional material you do have to address this basic concept first because it enables you to write much more pertinent letters if you understand who your target audience is and what they will respond to.

The press release

The press release is really an informative letter without the conventional layout of a letter. It is usually sent to newspapers, magazines, periodicals, radio and television stations – any area of the media that may be interested in the subject matter of the press release. Even though you have narrowed down the target market to just the media, it can be narrowed down even further. For example, if you are sending out a press release about your company's new computer training software, then you would target business publications and programmes, specifically those concerned with computers, science or technology.

It is important to decide what market you are addressing because it will determine what language you will use. For computer and technology publications and programmes you can use sophisticated technical language and give far more technical detail in the press release. For the straightforward business media you may choose to leave out some of the technical information and concentrate on the user-friendly qualities of your product.

The main point of a press release is to spread the news about your product or service. Any media that receive it may only have a small amount of space or time in which to refer to your product or service so you need to encapsulate all the newsworthy information in the first paragraph of your release. For example:

NEW DIY COMPUTER TRAINING COURSE

Sending staff on training courses is a thing of the past, thanks to the new Computer Wizard Training Software from IKO. Guaranteed to teach anyone anything and everything they need to know about computers in twelve half -hour sessions on their own computer, the Computer Wizard saves companies both time and money.

Figure 20: A typical press release (opening paragraph)

After the opening paragraph you can go on to explain in greater detail how the product or service works. Most media editors will only read the first paragraph to see whether the release is newsworthy. If you do not grab their attention in the first paragraph it will be thrown in the bin.

The main body of the release should be about the fine details of the product or service. Do not make this too long. It would be better to make your press release one page only and put contact details at the bottom in case the reader requires further information.

In this case, put a contact name and number at the bottom of the page so that journalists can request further details or pictures, or ask questions. Make sure that the contact person is constantly available, knows everything about the product and can either speak on behalf of the company or has strict instructions to limit his or her interaction with journalists and pass any difficult questions on to a senior person in the company.

A typical press release might be as follows:

NEW MOTORISED SKATEBOARD WILL BE HOTTEST TOY OF 2001!

AMICAL Toys Ltd. have developed a new motorised skateboard which will be in the shops in November 2000 ready for the Christmas rush.

The first of its kind, it retails at £39.99 and comes complete with shoulder and elbow pads and safety helmet. It has a concealed 5hp engine which will give an average cruising speed of 10 miles per hour. This is a rechargeable engine that plugs into a household mains supply and requires eight hours of charging to provide two hours of active skateboarding.

'We are confident that this product will be the biggest-selling toy this Christmas,' says William Avery, Managing Director of AMICAL.

AMICAL has had great success in the past three years by concentrating on rechargeable motorised toys. Last year, their motorised roller skates were a top seller, with seventeen million pairs sold worldwide.

For further information, photos and sample products please contact:
Marjorie Wilkinson, Sales Director, AMICAL
Tel : 09723 81914
Fax: 09723 88821
E-mail: Marj@AMICAL

Figure 21: A typical press release (entire text)

The sales letter

These tend to be personalised letters to named individuals, otherwise they do not perform any sales function at all. With the facilities available in word-processing software these days, it is possible to set up a standard letter that merely has to be 'topped and tailed' – that is, the recipient's name and address and your signature have to be added to each letter.

Again, the main sales pitch has to be in the first paragraph of the letter, otherwise it will be thrown away. The detail that follows has to be succinct and punchy. It is preferable to keep the letter to one page in length . The letter should close with an invitation to make contact if the recipient is interested in the product or service.

A common way of opening a sales letter is with a question. That question has to be central to the perceived need of the potential customer. Here are some examples of how a carefully targetted sales letter might start:

Dear Mr Gordon,
Is your central heating system old and unreliable?
Or
Dear Mr Gordon,
Are you paying too much for your electricity supply?
Or
Dear Mr Gordon,
Do you have poor television reception?
Or
Dear Mr Gordon,
Do you have a much-loved pet?

The answer to all the above questions should be yes, because the company sending out the sales letters should know from their research that Mr Gordon has either an old and unreliable central heating system, an expensive electricity supply, poor television reception or a much-loved pet. They will have been able to glean this information from various sources, mostly from records of purchases Mr Gordon has made -- particularly if he pays for things by credit card. So the opening question will be very relevant to Mr Gordon: the remaining task in the sales letter is to persuade him to part with his money to buy the product being promoted.

The rest of the sales letter will be devoted to explaining the product or service on offer, explaining the advantages of it and then telling him the price. This is usually saved until last because money is often a sticking point and you want Mr Gordon to really want the product before he finds out how much it will cost. A typical sales letter might be as follows:

(Usually on preprinted headed paper)

12 February 2000
Mr G Gordon
12 Aviary Walk
HENDON
Gloucestershire
GL7 3DS

Dear Mr Gordon,

Do you suffer with poor television reception, like others in your area? Are you limited to only one ITV channel and cannot get Channel 5 at all? Is your BBC2 picture often fuzzy, depending on the weather conditions?

If so, then you will definitely be interested in our new product, the Universal Indoor Aerial. It is guaranteed to give you crystal clear reception on any channel and can also provide reception of at least two ITV channels, depending on your location.

Outdoor aerials are often affected by weather conditions or can be knocked off position by birds or strong winds and it is impractical for most householders to go out onto their roofs to reposition their aerial. The attractive slimline Universal Indoor Aerial sits discreetly on top of your television or in any convenient position in your living room and will improve your television reception enormously.

The Universal Indoor Aerial costs £115.00. Buy two and the price goes down to £97.00 each; or for three or more, we can allow a further discount to £88.00 each! All come with a full life-time guarantee, and the option to return for a full refund if you are not entirely satisfied.

To order, simply complete the enclosed form and send with your remittance in the enclosed prepaid envelope. We will despatch your aerials by overnight courier, so there will be no need to wait for better reception!

Happy viewing,

G Connit
Connit Universal Aerials Ltd

You can see that this sales letter has asked several questions at the beginning: the answer to all of them should be yes. This is the foot in the door. Then the disadvantages of outdoor aerials are outlined. These are well known: Mr Gordon will identify with them. Then the advantages of the indoor aerial are outlined. Mr Gordon, by now, should be very interested. By the time the money is mentioned, we hope that Mr Gordon is so interested he won't flinch too much at the price and will consider ordering.

Other promotional material

You may choose to send out less formal promotional material – something that is not in letter form but takes the form of a fax, e-mail or just a promotional leaflet. Before doing so, note that many companies are getting tough on unwarranted intrusions, particularly in the case of promotional e-mail and faxes. They regard these promotional communications as interrupting important business communications (which they do), so often install junk safeguards on their computers and fax machines to eliminate the promotional stuff as soon as it reaches the target.

APPENDIX 1

Ceremonious forms of address

The Queen

Address: Her Majesty the Queen
Begin: Madam
With my humble duty
or
May it please Your Majesty
End: I have the honour to remain (or to be)
Madam
Your Majesty's most humble and obedient servant
or
Your Majesty's faithful subject

A royal prince

Address: His Royal Highness, the Prince of ...
or
His Royal Highness, Prince (the Prince's Christian name)
or (if the prince is a duke)
His Royal Highness, the Duke of ...
Begin: Sir
End: I have the honour to remain (or to be)
Sir
Your Royal Highness's most humble and obedient servant
or
Your Royal Highness's most dutiful subject

A royal princess

Address: Her Royal Highness, the Princess of ...
or
Her Royal Highness, Princess (the Princess' Christian name)
or (if the princess is a duchess)
Her Royal Highness, the Duchess of ...

Begin: Madam (whether married or not)
End: I have the honour to remain (or to be)
Madam
Your Royal Highness's most humble and obedient servant
or
Your Royal Highness's most dutiful subject

A duke

Address: His Grace the Duke of ...
Begin: My Lord Duke
End: I have the honour to be, Your Grace's most obedient servant
or
Respectfully

A duchess

Address: Her Grace the Duchess of ...
Begin: Madam
End: I have the honour to be, Your Grace's most obedient servant
or
Respectfully

A marquess, earl, viscount, baron (peers other than a duke)

Address: The Most Hon the Marquess of ...
The Rt Hon the Earl of ...
The Rt Hon the Viscount ....
The Rt Hon the Lord ...
Begin: My Lord
End: I am, sir, your obedient servant
or
Yours faithfully

The wife of a peer other than a duke

Address: The Most Hon the Marchioness of ....
The Rt Hon the Countess of ...
The Rt Hon the Viscountess ...
The Rt Hon the Baroness ....
Begin: Dear Madam
End: I am, Madam, your obedient servant
or
Yours faithfully

A baronet

Address: Sir (Christian name and surname) Bt.
Begin: Dear Sir
End: Your obedient servant
or
Yours faithfully

The wife of a baronet

Address: Lady (surname only)
Begin: Dear Madam
End: Your obedient servant
or
Yours faithfully

A knight

Address: Sir (Christian name and surname)
With appropriate letters after the name for example KCB
Begin: Dear Sir
End: Yours faithfully

The wife of a knight

Address: Lady (surname only)
Begin: Dear Madam
End: Yours faithfully

An archbishop

Address: The Most Reverend, the Lord Archbishop of ...
Begin: Dear Archbishop
End: Yours sincerely

A bishop

Address: The Right Reverend the Lord Bishop of ...
Begin: Dear Bishop
End: Yours sincerely

A dean

Address: The Very Reverend the Dean of ...
Begin: Dear Dean
End: Yours sincerely

An archdeacon

Address: The Venerable the Archdeacon of ...
Begin: Dear Archdeacon
End: Yours sincerely

An ambassador (British)

Address: His Excellency (rank) H.B.M's Ambassador and Plenipotentiary
Begin: Sir, My Lord etc. according to rank
or
Your Excellency
End: I have the honour to be, sir
Your Excellency's obedient servant

A governor general or governor

Address: His excellency (Christian name and surname) Governor General of ....
or
His excellency (Christian name and surname) Governor of ....
Begin: Sir
or
Your Excellency
or
My Lord (if a peer)
End : I have the honour to be, sir (or My Lord)
Your Excellency's obedient servant

A consul general

Address: (Full name) Esq. H.B.M's Consul General
(also same for Consul or Vice Consul)
Begin: Sir
End: Sir, I am your obedient servant

A member of Her Majesty's Government

A letter sent to a Minister as the head of his department is addressed by his appointment only, for example:
Address: The Secretary of State for ...
Begin: Dear Sir
End: Yours faithfully

If the writer knows the Minister concerned, it is permissible to write to him or her by the name of his or her appointment, for example:
Begin: Dear Prime Minister
Dear Lord Privy Seal
Dear Chancellor
End: Yours sincerely

If writing to a Member of Parliament then:
Address: Mr/Mrs or Ms or other title (full name) M.P.
Begin: Dear Sir/Madam/Lord
End: Yours faithfully

A lord mayor

Address: The Right Honourable the Lord Mayor of ... *(see below)
Begin: My Lord Mayor
End: Yours faithfully
(*The title 'The Right Honourable' can only be given to the Lord Mayors of London, York, Belfast and Dublin. All other Lord Mayors are referred to as 'The Right Worshipful the Lord Mayor of ...')

An alderman

Address: Alderman (followed by any title or rank and full name)
Begin: My Lord, Dear Sir, Dear Madam or Dear Alderman (according to personal rank)
End: Yours faithfully

A councillor

Address: Councillor (followed by any title or rank and full name)
Begin: My Lord, Dear Sir, Dear Madam or Dear Councillor (according to personal rank)
End: Yours faithfully

APPENDIX 2

Troublesome words and phrases

Commonly misspelled or misused words

The following pairs of words sound the same and are often mixed up. We have shown the correct meanings in parentheses. Make sure you use the correct word for the meaning you intend to convey.

accept (receive)	except (omit, excluding)
affect (influence)	effect (result)
all ready (entirely prepared)	already (previously)
allusion (reference)	illusion (false impression) elusion (escape)
appraise (value or estimate)	apprise (inform, learn)
baring (uncovering)	bearing (carrying, withstanding)
biannual (twice a year)	biennial (every two years)
capital (city or letter)	capitol (building)
complement (complete or alternative)	compliment (praise or respect)
council (meeting)	counsel (advice)
dependent (to depend upon something or someone – the adjective)	dependant (something or someone that is dependent – the noun)
dyeing (colouring)	dying (near death)
eminent (important)	imminent (forthcoming)
enquiry (question)	inquiry (investigation)
formally (in a formal way)	formerly (at an earlier time)
forth (forward)	fourth (after third)
licence (the noun)	license (the verb)
miner (mine worker)	minor (lesser or smaller, or a juvenile)
personal (private)	personnel (staff)
prescribe (order)	proscribe (prohibit)
principal (most important, or the headmaster of a school)	principle (standard of conduct or truth)
stationary (immobile)	stationery (writing supplies)
weather (rain or sun etc)	whether (conjunction)

Other misused words

In addition to the homophones (similar-sounding words) previously listed, the following pairs of words are often confused, but again their meanings are not identical. If you are not sure of their different meanings consult a dictionary.

aggravate	annoy
alternatively	alternately
anticipate	expect
appreciate	realise
appropriate	relevant
bankrupt	insolvent
comprise	compose
continuous	continual
disinterested	uninterested
imply	infer
learn	teach
practical	practicable

Alternatives to long or complex words

The following words are unnecessarily long or complicated. Use the shorter version instead – it makes your writing much clearer.

accomplish	do
acquaint	tell
acquiesce	agree
acquire	get, gain
approximately	about
ascertain	find out
come to a decision	decide
commence	begin, start
communicate	write, phone
consequent upon	after
considerable	much
considerable period	long time
currently	now
dearth	lack
despatch	send
donate	give
due to the fact that	because, as
endeavour	try
experience	feel
facilitate	make easier
forward	send
inform	tell
in the course of	during
in the event of	if
in the meantime	meanwhile
in the near future	soon

locality	place
majority	most
materialise	take place
on behalf of	for
on the question of	about
peruse	read
proximity	near
purchase	buy
remunerate	pay, reward
requirements	needs
shall take steps to	shall
transmit	send
terminate	end
utilise	use
with regard to	about
with the object of	to

Alternatives to clichés

Clichés should be avoided wherever possible, especially in letters to foreign readers or where translation is required, as they often make no literal sense. The alternative is usually shorter, and far clearer to your reader. Where 'omit' is shown, just remove the cliché completely.

assuring you of our best attention	(omit)
at this moment in time	now
at your earliest convenience	as soon as possible
be that as it may	(omit)
enclosed herewith	I enclose, I am enclosing
furnish particulars	give details
hereto	(avoid by rewording sentence)
I await the pleasure of a reply	I look forward to hearing from you
increased consumer resistance has been encountered	sales have dropped
inst	(use month name instead)
of even date	of today
ongoing	continuing
owing to unforeseen circumstances	unexpectedly
per	by
re your letter	with reference to your letter
prox	(omit)
the favour of your early reply will oblige	I shall be glad to hear from you soon
ult	(omit)
we are desirous of	we want
we beg to inform you	we are writing to let you know
we take pleasure in advising	we are pleased to let you know
your letter has come to hand	your letter has arrived
your goodself	you

APPENDIX 3

Punctuation and typing correction marks

,	comma
;	semicolon
:	colon
.	period or full stop
!	exclamation mark
?	question mark
-	hyphen
'	apostrophe
( )	parentheses
[ ]	brackets
}	brace (to enclose two or more lines)
´	acute accent as in blasé
`	grave accent as in crème
^	circumflex accent as in tête
~	tilde, a Spanish accent, as in señor
¸	cedilla, as in façade
' '	quotation marks (also speech marks)
" "	marks for quotes within quotes
¨	umlaut, a German accent, as in Köln
—	em dash
–	en dash
©	copyright
®	Registered
™	Trademark
§	section
¶	paragraph
...	ellipsis
%	per cent
&	ampersand, and
&c	etcetera
*	asterisk
#	number, space
†	dagger, a reference mark
‡	double dagger, another reference mark
⅄	caret, insertion mark

Index